ON FOOT ON
WEST SUSSEX DOWNS

*18 short, medium and long walks
in West Sussex*

BEN PERKINS

S.B. Publications

By the same author

South Downs: Walks for Motorists
Pub Walks in the South Downs
Village Walks in East Sussex
Waterside Walks in Sussex
Sussex Border Path: Guide and Map Pack
On Foot on the East Sussex Downs
Pub Strolls in East Sussex
Pub Strolls in West Sussex
Classic Walks in Sussex

Contributed walks to:

Walkers Britain and Walkers Britain 2
AA Book of Village Walks
Exploring Britain's Long Distance Paths
AA Book of Family Walks

First published in 2002 by S.B. Publications
19 Grove Road, Seaford, East Sussex BN25 1TP
Tel: 01323 893498

ISBN 1 85770 251 4

Typeset by EH Graphics, East Sussex (01273) 515527
Printed by Tansleys Printers, Seaford (01323) 891019

CONTENTS

ACKNOWLEDGMENTS

The Author is indebted to the Society of Sussex Downsmen and Harry Comber for the use of part of the title of their original publication 'On Foot in East Sussex', now out of print.
Also, special thanks to John Barnes and Brian Ellis who accompanied me on many of the walks and for their help with route finding.

INTRODUCTION

This book is a companion volume to 'On Foot on the East Sussex Downs' published in 2000. However, walking on the downs in West Sussex offers a completely different and varied experience even though the chalk underlying the whole length of the South Downs does, to an extent, determine and unify the character of the landscape. Large areas of the West Sussex downs are heavily wooded in striking contrast to the, largely, bare hills to the east of the River Adur where most of the traditional 19th Century sheep walks were once located. Although much of this woodland, particularly on the southern dip slope of the Downs, is modern afforestation, there are patches of older woodland such as on Newtimber Hill (Walk 1) and Watergate Hanger (Walk 17).

The two wide river valleys carved by the Arun and the Adur, the only two breaks in the 80-mile length of the South Downs, offer opportunities for fine views from the flanking hills (Walks 3, 8, 9 and 13). The extensive area of rolling hills and valleys to the northwest of Chichester, where the Downs are at their widest from north to south, is as remote as anywhere in this overcrowded corner of England (Walks 6, 12 and 17). Add to this the dramatic northern escarpment (Walks 4 and 7), several lovely old downland churches such as at Sullington (Walk 2), East Dean (Walk 16) and Up Marden (Walk 17), and fine ancient earthworks like the Trundle (Walk 11) and the Devil's Jumps (Walk 12) and you have a landscape of unsurpassed richness and variety.

The new book follows the same format as its East Sussex companion. The longer circuits (Walks 13 to 18) offer an overview of the West Sussex Downs, enough to provide a week of full day walks, while the shorter half day walks fill in some gaps and also visit some rather special areas such as Arundel Park (Walk 3) and the outlying downland hills of Newtimber and Wolstonbury (Walk 1). Some of the shorter or medium circuits might also be combined, without significant overlap (Walks 7 and 8 or Walks 6 and 12 are easily linked). The walk descriptions and the accompanying sketch maps should be detailed enough, between them, to guide you round the walks but I would not recommend setting out without a copy of the appropriate OS Explorer Map. Features on the ground change over time, signs disappear, paths are occasionally diverted, and if you do happen to stray off the described route, a map becomes essential. A map will also help you get to the start and allow you to orientate yourself in relation to features in the surrounding countryside. Luckily, most of the downland paths are well established underfoot and well maintained and signed under the supervision of the Sussex Downs Conservation Board.

Getting to the start of many of the walks presents problems if you are reliant on public transport. Although most of the starting points are accessible only by car, many of the routes can be joined at other points using bus services along the main roads through the Downs. For details of bus routes and times, telephone the West Sussex County Council 'Traveline' - 0870 6082608.

The hills of the South Downs have led a precarious existence over the last 50 years since they were extensively ploughed during World War II. Their importance as a landscape of both local and national significance is well recognised but only 3% of the area remains as traditional chalk downland and the decline continues. There are, however, hopeful signs. Under the Environmentally Sensitive Area scheme, 6000 acres of arable land is being allowed to revert to grassland and other arable reversion schemes are planned. In spite of entrenched resistance from the County Councils of both East and West Sussex, designation of the South Downs as a National Park is now well under way and should eventually strengthen the environmental management of this glorious, but vulnerable countryside.

Re-visiting the West Sussex Downs in a systematic way during the preparation of these walks has been a delight. I hope you will get the same enjoyment by following in my footsteps.

B.P.

If you would like to help protect the Sussex Downs, why not join the only independent organisation exclusively concerned with the preservation of the Downs. For more details of the Society of Sussex Downsmen, contact the Secretary at 10, The Drive, Hove, East Sussex, BN3 3JA (Telephone: 01273 771906)

LOCATION OF WALKS

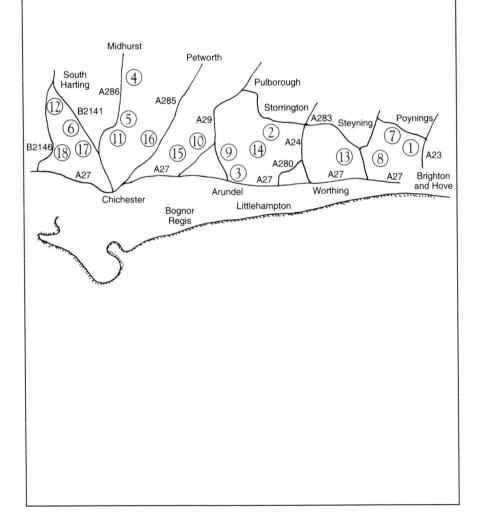

Walk 1
NEWTIMBER HILL AND WOLSTONBURY HILL

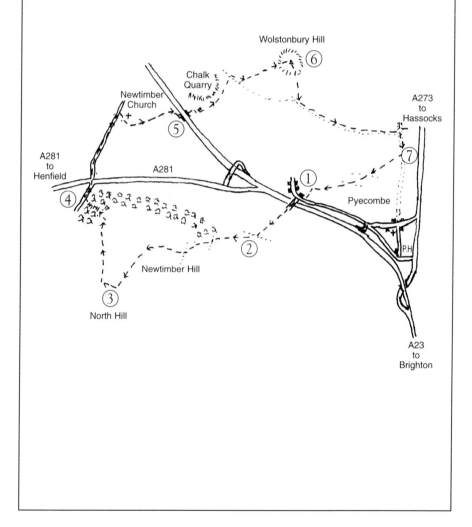

Walk 1

NEWTIMBER HILL AND WOLSTONBURY HILL

Distance:	4¹/₂ miles.
Route:	Pyecombe - Newtimber Hill - Newtimber Church - Wolstonbury Hill - Pyecombe.
Map:	OS Explorer 122: South Downs Way - Steyning to Newhaven.
Start/Parking:	Towards the far end of the redundant section of the old A23 at Pyecombe, accessible northbound from the A273 and southbound from the new A23, just north of the junction of the two roads north of Brighton. Park at GR 284128.
Public Transport:	Bus from Brighton to Pyecombe Garage, close to the start.
Conditions:	A short but fairly strenuous walk with two climbs and one very steep descent. Good tracks or downland/field paths. One short stretch along a quiet lane.
Refreshments:	None on the walk. Plough Inn at Pyecombe, a quarter mile from the start.

In spite of the close proximity of the busy A23, the twin hills of Newtimber and Wolstonbury are two of the finest hills on the Sussex Downs, each standing partially separated from the main escarpment and instantly recognisable from afar - Newtimber clothed in trees and Wolstonbury, bare and shapely. Starting from Pyecombe, this walk visits both summits, each at over 650 ft above sea level, where you can wander freely, thanks to the National Trust who now own and manage much of the area explored on this walk. The only snag is in the form of the busy and noisy A23 which has to be crossed twice on the walk (luckily bridges over and under the dual carriageway have been provided since the A23 was upgraded).

Although fairly short in length, allow plenty of time not only to savour the many delights but also to tackle the steep ups and downs at a steady pace.

THE WALK

*From the far end of the segment of old road **(1)**, just past Pyecombe House and a telephone box on your right, turn left across a footbridge over the new A23. A few yards beyond the bridge, go ahead along a signed bridleway which passes through two gates and commences a steady climb up on to the Downs along the left edge of pasture. In the field corner, where you have a choice of signed paths ahead, go through a gap and fork right, still climbing steadily, now along a right field edge.*

*After 250 yards go through a gate **(2)** where a notice indicates that you are entering the National Trust area of Newtimber Hill. Immediately beyond the gate, sidestep to the left up a low bank and turn right along the right edge of an open grassy area with a scrub and tree covered slope dropping away to the right. In the field corner go through another gate and veer slightly left on a faint path which heads generally westwards across the flat summit area of Newtimber Hill passing through a patchwork of grass, scrub and small trees.*

The views are disappointing at first but, as you proceed, a wide vista opens up ahead along the escarpment of the Downs between Devil's Dyke and Chanctonbury Ring.

Poynings village and the Western Downs from Newtimber Hill.

View back to Newtimber Hill from shoulder of Wolstonbury Hill,

The path veers left and descends into a shallow dip between Newtimber Hill and North Hill. At the lowest point in the dip **(3)** turn squarely right. Very shortly the ground begins to drop away ahead and the village of Poynings with its prominent square-towered church comes into view directly ahead at the foot of the slope. About a third of the way down the hill turn right on a faint but trodden path which contours along the hillside without gaining or losing much height.

A few yards after the path curves to the right round the shoulder of the hill and Wolstonbury comes into sight ahead, turn left on a worn path which drops very steeply down the hill (take care - slippery!) to enter woodland over a stile. Now, assisted in places by steps, follow a clear path down through the wood. Ignoring a path, signed 'Woodland', heading back to the right, continue down through the wood to join a lane **(4)** and turn right.

Cross the A281 and follow the lane, signposted to Newtimber Church, opposite. After about 500 yards **(5)** turn right into the churchyard, passing to the right of the church. Leave the churchyard through a swing gate and turn left along a left field edge. In the field corner go through a gap and ahead along a right field edge, then right to join a road and immediately left beneath the A23 **(5)**.

After another 100 yards or so go right along a concrete drive and shortly left over a stile and along a narrow path which skirts to the right of farm buildings and climbs through scrub, with an active chalk quarry to your left. A steeper climb leads up across grass to a stile. Turn left along a track for five yards then right through a gate.

Bear right along a well-trodden bridleway and after about 150 yards go left along an unfenced grassy path which soon climbs within a gully through an area of old grass covered quarry workings. At a fence go right beside it until you can go left over a stile in this fence and climb up to the summit of Wolstonbury Hill (6).

For the best views, allow time for a complete circuit of the low grass covered rampart of the Iron Age Fort which encircles the summit. Walking clockwise you can admire, in turn, the view back to Newtimber Hill and the western Downs, a wide Wealden panorama to the north, the twin windmills of Jack and Jill against a backdrop of Ditchling Beacon to the east and a glimpse of Brighton and the sea to the south.

From the trig point on the summit follow a trodden path which heads approximately southwards, over the rampart and on across grass for 100 yards or so to join a fenced

View west from Newtimber Hill.

track between low wooden posts. Turn left up to a gate on the skyline and on with a fence, right, soon aiming directly for Jack and Jill on the hill opposite. At a crossing track where several ways meet, turn squarely right along a fenced path. After about 150 yards **(7)** turn right over a stile and follow an unfenced path over the shoulder of a hill and down to a stile. Descend to a second stile and continue obliquely down across pasture to a third stile. Bear right for a few yards across a farmyard and then go left over a stile from which a short enclosed path leads out via a house access drive to join the old A23 within yards of the start.

Walk 2
KITHURST HILL AND SULLINGTON

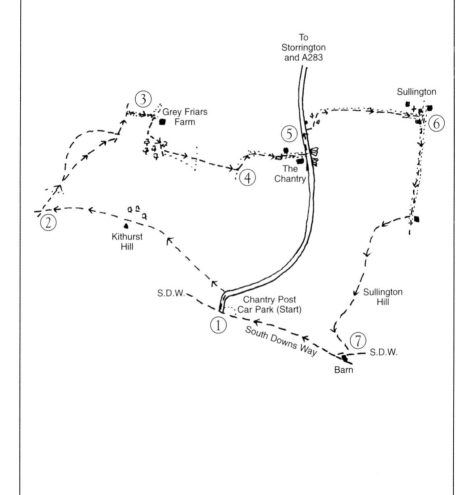

To
Storrington
and A283

Sullington

③

Grey Friars
Farm

⑤

⑥

④

The
Chantry

②

Kithurst
Hill

S.D.W.

Sullington
Hill

Chantry Post
Car Park (Start)

①

South Downs Way

⑦

S.D.W.

Barn

Walk 2

KITHURST HILL AND SULLINGTON

Distance:	4¹/₂ miles
Route:	Chantry Post - Kithurst Hill - Grey Friars Farm - Sullington - Sullington Hill - Chantry Post.
Map:	OS Explorer 121: Arundel and Pulborough.
Start/Parking:	From the A283 just east of Storrington, follow Chantry Lane southwards, signposted to The Downs. Park in the Chantry Post car park on the summit of the Downs at GR 087119.
Public Transport:	None convenient
Conditions:	Generally good, along clear paths or tracks but may be muddy in places, particularly where some of the tracks have been churned up by heavy equestrian use.
Refreshments:	None on route.

Some of the best walking on the South Downs can be found when exploring the paths which allow access up and down the steep northern escarpment. Many of these paths follow ancient routes, often as grassy terraces or deep hollow ways which were established to link the high pastures with the settlements at the foot of the Downs. Rarer are the occasional paths which contour along the side of the scarp slope, one of which we are able to use on this walk.

Starting with a high traverse over the 700 ft summit of Kithurst Hill, we soon plunge down through woodland before picking a way along the lower downland slopes to reach the delightful hamlet of Sullington. A steady climb, much of it across undulating open downland brings us back up to join the South Downs Way which we can follow back to the start.

Although short, it is a fairly strenuous walk so allow plenty of time to complete it. A good two hours should suffice, adding on time to linger and admire the views.

THE WALK

From the Chantry Post car park *(1)* start the walk back down the road by which you approached the Downs. After a little over 100 yards, before you have lost much height, turn sharply back to the left along a signed bridleway which climbs gently but steadily up to the highest point on Kithurst Hill with fine views northwards across the Weald.

From the trig point on the summit, the view northwards is partially obscured by trees, but an equally fine view opens out southwards across the uneven dip slope of the Downs to the coastal plain and the sea. On a good day the Isle of Wight is clearly visible.

Beyond the summit a clear track continues along the escarpment. After another quarter of a mile *(2)* turn sharply back to the right along a fenced track which soon enters woodland and drops steadily down the scarp slope. About half way down, where you have a choice of waymarked routes, either will do as they rejoin lower down. Both are severely poached and eroded, but the one to the right may be slightly preferable. Whichever route you choose, at the bottom of the hill bear left along a wide track and, after about 150 yards, turn right, still on a clear access track.

On reaching the entrance to Grey Friars Farm on your right *(3)* turn right into the drive and immediately fork right again along an enclosed tree-lined path, doubling back on your previous direction and heading towards the Downs. At the foot of the steep escarpment bear left with the main track and, after 100 yards or so, at a waypost, fork right, still on a clear track which climbs between banks.

After less than 100 yards, fork left through a gate and head out across a field with

View from the start of the walk near Chantry Post.

a fence on your right at first, contouring along the hillside with little gain or loss in height. Go over a stile in a crossing fence and maintain direction to a second stile (4). Now bear left, dropping down. In the bottom field corner bear right through two gates and go forward along a left field edge and on along a farm access drive to join a lane opposite two large ornamental ponds.

Turn left along the lane. Just past a tiny waterfall on your right (5) turn right through a gate, go forward past a cottage then left through the second of two gates on your left. A well trodden and ridden path climbs obliquely up a wooded bank and continues beside fields to reach the tiny hamlet of Sullington. As you approach the first house go forward through a gate and along an access drive passing Sullington Church on your left.

The tiny settlement of Sullington consists of little more than manor house and farm clustered round the tiny church. The farm is notable for a 17th century tithe barn with impressive timber roof beams and the manor house faces directly on to the churchyard. The church is of Saxon origins with many later additions including an interesting variety of stained glass windows, ancient and modern, and a heavily vandalised but still impressive marble effigy of a knight crusader.

At a junction of tracks just beyond the church (6) turn right and head for the Downs along a wide track. After a little over a quarter of a mile, just short of a flint barn, fork right along a track which climbs across open downland, unfenced between low banks at first. Continue with this track as it bears left, climbing steadily up on to Sullington Hill and on to join the South Downs Way (7) about 100 yards to the left of a barn, prominently visible on the skyline. Turn right along the South Downs Way, passing to the right of this barn and continuing along a clear track back to the start at Chantry Post.

Sullington Church

17

Walk 3
ARUNDEL PARK

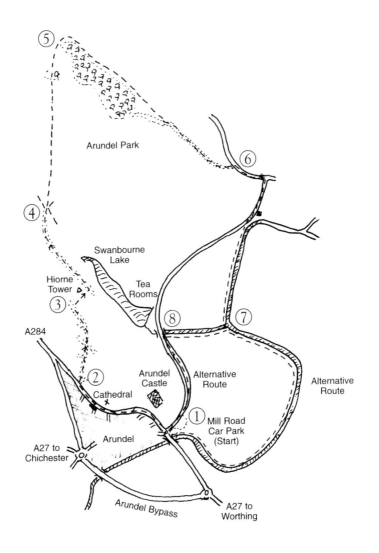

Walk 3

ARUNDEL PARK

Distance:	4¹/₂ miles
Route:	Arundel - Arundel Park - Offham - Black Rabbit pub - Arun river bank - Mill Road - Arundel.
Map:	OS Explorer 121: Arundel and Pulborough
Start/Parking:	Beside Mill Road, Arundel (free) or in the Mill Road Car Park (Fee payable) at the bottom of the town at GR 020071.
Public Transport:	Train or bus to Arundel.
Conditions:	Road through Arundel, then on good paths and tracks or across open parkland and along riverside paths.
Refreshments:	Pubs and tea rooms in Arundel. Black Rabbit pub at Offham.

Although the town of Arundel is a honey-pot for tourists during the summer months, few venture far into the 1200 rolling acres of Arundel Park where you can wander freely except on one day (24th March) each year. Our walk climbs steadily up through the park to reach a fine viewpoint overlooking the Arun valley, well away from the crowds. The return route descends into the valley and, after passing the conveniently placed Black Rabbit pub, beautifully situated beside the river, offers options for shorter or longer walks beside the River Arun, back into Arundel.

The town is dominated by the Castle, the family seat of the Dukes of Norfolk and is open to the public every day except Saturday from April to October. Also worth visiting are the Roman Catholic Cathedral, built in 1870 in French Gothic style and the more modest Parish Church, nearby. There is also a small museum of local history in the High Street.

THE WALK

From the Mill Road Car Park *(1)*, *return to the mini-roundabout at the bottom of the town and turn right up the High Street, following it round to the left beneath the walls of Arundel Castle and on past the parish church on the right and the Roman Catholic Cathedral on the left. About 200 yards past the cathedral (2), fork right along the main drive into Arundel Park and follow it for half a mile up, through a stone gateway and on into the park, ignoring all side turnings. At a waypost (3), turn squarely right across grass, passing about 60 yards to the right of the Hiorne Tower.*

Strikingly situated on one of the higher points in the park, this triangular building with castellated turrets at each corner was designed by a certain Francis Hiorne and built in 1790.

Cross a gallop, go forward downhill on a narrow path and then turn left over a stile beside a gate to follow a track which contours along the hill side and then drops obliquely down into a beautiful sheltered combe. At the bottom of the hill, where a

Arundel Castle from Arundel river bank.

Hiorne Tower, Arundel Park.

number of ways meet **(4)**, you should follow the direction of a yellow arrow on a post ahead up a steep slope where a narrow path has been trodden out. At the top of this short, sharp incline, go over a stile in a fence and continue in the same direction, climbing more gently across open grassland. There is no defined path but you are free to walk anywhere.

Go over a stile beside a clump of trees and ahead to reach the left hand end of a long band of trees **(5)**. The signed footpath goes ahead here but you should bear right following the wood edge through a gate, curving round and back along the ridge with the trees on your right.

From this superb vantage point a magnificent view opens out, northwards into the Weald, southwards to Arundel Castle and the coastal plain and, in between, a wide sweep of the valley of the Arun with glimpses of the river as it encircles the small hamlet of South Stoke with its tiny church, set against a backdrop of the Downs, rising up on the eastern side of the valley.

Follow a clear track to another gate at the far end of the long strip of woodland and then go forward across open downland. Join a more substantial chalk and flint track coming in from behind on the right and follow it obliquely down into the valley and out of the Park on to a lane through an imposing gateway crowned by carved effigies of a lion and unicorn **(6)**.

Go ahead along the lane and, at a road junction, turn right, dropping down between high tree-lined banks. About 30 yards past the access to the Black Rabbit, an

Arundel Park.

attractively set riverside pub, turn left along the edge of the pub car park and forward along a path which follows the raised right bank of the River Arun downstream, though the river is largely hidden behind reeds.

After almost a half a mile you will come to a path junction **(7)** *where you have a choice. If time and energy permit, carry on along the river bank which takes you in a wide loop back to Arundel, a distance of a little over a mile. For a shorter route back to the start, turn right along a narrow path between two reed filled ditches. It brings you out on to Mill Road* **(8)**.

A short detour to the right from here brings you to Swanbourne Lake, a popular tourist picnic spot, with tea rooms and rowing boats for hire during the summer months. Fed by underground springs, the lake has had a precarious existence in recent years, drying out on more than one occasion following excessive water abstraction.

Turn left along a tree-lined path beside Mill Road, back to the start.

Arundel Castle.

Walk 4
HEYSHOTT DOWN AND COCKING

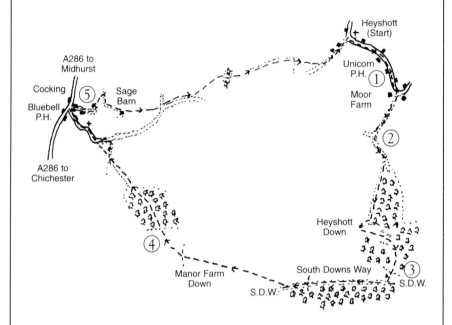

Cocking Church.

Walk 4

HEYSHOTT DOWN AND COCKING

Distance:	4¹/₄ miles
Route:	Heyshott - Heyshott Down - South Downs Way - Manor Farm Down - Cocking - Heyshott.
Map:	OS Explorer 120: Chichester and OS Explorer 121: Arundel and Pulborough.
Start/Parking:	At the village of Heyshott, most easily accessible along unclassified roads from the A286 Midhurst-to-Chichester road about a mile north of Cocking. There is roadside parking in the vicinity of the Unicorn Inn at GR 899179.
Public Transport:	None
Conditions:	The walk follows good paths throughout. One short steep climb requires care and some agility and there is one sharp and potentially slippery descent.
Refreshments:	Unicorn Inn at Heyshott. Bluebell Inn at Cocking.

The highlight of this walk is the Heyshott Down Escarpment Nature Reserve, a superb area of chalk downland which is gradually being created within an area of disused quarry workings on the steep northern slope of the Downs above Heyshott. Managed by the Murray Downland Trust, the area is being selectively cleared of scrub and grazed, the aim being to restore and recreate a habitat rich in wild flowers. The path through the reserve used on the walk is not marked on OS maps but is stiled to provide a practicable route, though it is very steep in one or two places. After a short walk along part of the South Downs Way, our route heads out across the open summit of Manor Farm Down with fine views. A steep descent through woodland brings us to the village of Cocking from which the return route uses field paths back to Heyshott.

THE WALK

From the Unicorn Inn *(1)* start the walk by continuing along the village street, soon heading directly towards the Downs. Where the metalled lane takes a sharp turn round to the left and you have a choice of two routes ahead, you should keep right along a roughly metalled track, signed as a No Through Road. Where this track divides, keep left and, after about 200 yards, beside a Nature Reserve notice, fork right past two low wooden posts *(2)*.

Follow a clear path up within the right edge of an area of scrub, now on a permissive route within the nature reserve. Where the slope steepens, bear right, climbing steeply with a fence on your left. After about 50 yards go left over a stile in this fence and bear left on a faint path which soon climbs steeply up through a hummocky area of old quarry workings before contouring left to another stile. A narrow path continues along the steep slope, gradually gaining height and passing a third stile, to arrive at a small plateau.

From this point there is a magnificent view northwards across the Weald with the radio mast on Bexley Hill clearly visible and, on a clear day, the heights of Blackdown.

From this plateau turn squarely right, steeply up a bank to join a higher contour path. Bear left along this path soon climbing sharply up a grassy bluff to reach a stile where there is another Nature Reserve notice. Beyond the stile where you leave the reserve, head squarely out across a field, passing a trig point and continuing to join a track *(3)*.

Turn right and follow this track, part of the South Downs Way. After a quarter of a mile, go straight over a crossing bridleway and, after less than 100 yards, at a five-armed signpost, fork half right across a large field where a faint trodden path is usually visible across the open summit of Manor Farm Down.

A view soon opens out - ahead to Cocking Down on the other side of a valley and southwards to St Roche's Hill (Walk 11) and a glimpse of the sea beyond.

Go over a stile in a crossing fence and veer slightly right, dropping down across the next field with the village of Cocking now in view directly ahead. The path enters woodland *(4)* and drops steeply down, where it may be slippery after rain. Leave the wood and continue down along a left field edge. Towards the bottom of the hill turn left over a stile. From here the path officially heads half right across a field to join a lane but may be destroyed by ploughing. If so you may find it easier to follow the right field headland out to the lane. Whichever route you follow turn left along the lane into Cocking, following it out to the A286.

The pub marked on the map at this point (The Bluebell Inn) has had a chequered existence. Closed until recently, it has, at the time of writing, re-opened for business.

To continue the walk, don't join the main road. Instead, just short of it, turn back to the right along Mill Lane **(5).** The lane becomes a track which, after crossing a millstream, bears left beside it. Where the track ends, a narrow path continues, soon at the foot of a steep scrub-covered bank with a garden on your left. At the far end of the garden, where the path divides, turn sharply right up some rudimentary steps doubling back on your previous direction, soon following a right field edge.

Skirt to the left of a house called Sages Barn and head squarely out across the field beyond. Cross a sunken track using two stiles and go forward along a right field edge, walking parallel to another sunken track on your right. At a finger post veer half left across the middle of a field where the path may be ploughed out. A waypost indicates the point of entry into a wood.

Follow a clear path through this small wood and on across the next field to pick up and follow a hedge on your left. Where this hedge ends at a plank bridge and stile, go directly ahead across the field beyond to join a metalled drive over a stile. Turn left and follow this drive back into Heyshott where you will join the village street opposite the church. Turn right back to the Unicorn Inn and the start.

The path down to Cocking.

Walk 5

LEVIN DOWN, SINGLETON AND CHARLTON

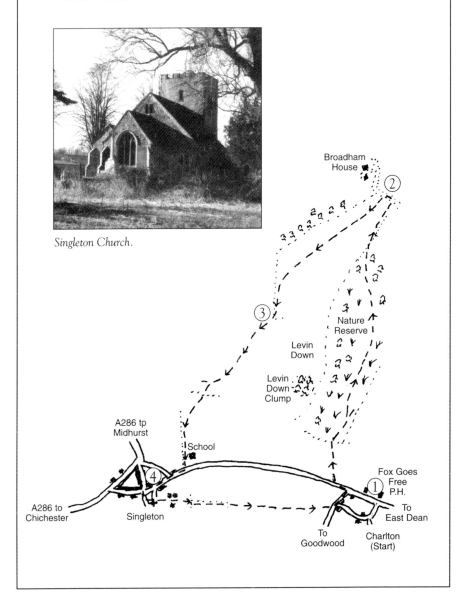

Singleton Church.

Broadham House

②

③

Nature Reserve

Levin Down

Levin Down Clump

A286 tp Midhurst

School

A286 to Chichester

Singleton

④

Fox Goes Free P.H.

①

To East Dean

To Goodwood

Charlton (Start)

Walk 5

LEVIN DOWN, SINGLETON AND CHARLTON

Distance:	3 miles
Route:	Charlton - Levin Down Nature Reserve - Broadham - Levin Down - Singleton - Charlton.
Map:	OS Explorer 120: Chichester
Start/Parking:	At the village of Charlton, a mile east along an unclassified road which leaves the A286 Chichester-to-Midhurst road at Singleton. There is room to park beside the road to the west of the Fox Goes Free pub or a few yards along the lane signposted to Goodwood. GR 888130
Public Transport:	None
Conditions:	Easy walking along good paths and across open downland.
Refreshments:	Fox Goes Free pub at Charlton, Fox and Hounds pub at Singleton.

The highlight of this short and generally easy circuit is an opportunity to enjoy an area which is specially protected as a designated Site of Special Scientific Interest and managed as a nature reserve by the Sussex Wildlife Trust. From the tiny settlement of Charlton, the walk climbs to enter and traverse the eastern slope of Levin Down within the reserve before turning to climb back over higher ground to the east, outside the reserve but, at the time of writing, still managed as permanent pasture and to which future access may be established under the open access provisions of the 2000 Countryside Act.

After dropping down into Singleton, a delightful unspoilt downland village with a welcoming pub, the return route follows a field path along the Lavant valley. The River Lavant is a winterbourne, normally dry, though liable to flooding during wet winters.

THE WALK

*From the road junction to the west of the Fox Goes Free pub **(1)** start the walk along the road signposted to Singleton and Midhurst. After about 50 yards go right over a stile and up across a field to enter Levin Down Nature Reserve. Just inside the Reserve, where there is a helpful information board, fork right, keeping a fence on your right. After less than 100 yards go over a stile by a gate and immediately fork left on a path which rises gently at first before contouring along the hillside through a patchy mixture of scrub, Juniper and chalk grass land.*

Levin Down, grazed and unploughed for centuries, is notable for a colony of Juniper trees and also an area of so-called 'chalk heath' where a mix of acid and alkali soils allow acid loving heather to grow and thrive alongside a wide range of chalk downland flowers. The warm south facing slope of the area also makes it an excellent butterfly habitat, supporting varieties such as the chalkhill blue and brown argus.

*A path eventually continues through thicker woodland. Leave the wood over a stile and continue along the right edge of a large open expanse of pasture. In the field corner go over a stile and forward for a few yards to join a chalk and flint track. Turn left and, after less than 100 yards **(2)** fork left, passing a few yards to the left of a solid oak post, inscribed 'Old Charlton Hunt'. It was once an elaborate signpost but has now lost all its arms. Go forward through a gate and head out gently uphill across the open grass land of Levin Down walking roughly parallel to trees, away to your right. As you cross the shoulder of the hill you should gradually converge on and then follow a fence on your right.*

A superb view opens out ahead across the valley towards St Roche's Hill, crowned by the earthworks of an Iron Age fort, The Trundle (Walk 11) and also twin radio masts. The skyline is also disfigured by the modern grandstand at Goodwood Racecourse, a hideously inappropriate blot on this lovely landscape.

*In the field corner **(3)** go through a gate and ahead on a faint unfenced path which soon curves to the right past an isolated fingerpost. After another 200 yards or so, at a*

The view from Levin Down.

second post, turn left, signposted to Singleton and drop down across grass to a stile, in sight. A path continues down the hill, across and beside a field and out past the village school to join a lane where you should turn right into Singleton village. Shortly, keep left. Just past the Fox and Hounds pub on your right **(4),** *turn left along a narrow lane. After 60 yards go left through a gate into Singleton churchyard.*

Flint cottages, Singleton

Although extensively rebuilt, the church retains a Saxon tower with a minstrels' gallery and the 13th Century chancel still has an old oak timbered roof. Many of the houses in the village are built with characteristic flint walls, some with thatched roofs.

Five yards inside the churchyard, go forward on a narrow path between wall and hedge. Go ahead through the small church car park. A path continues in a straight line, beside a meadow and on through an estate of relatively new houses. The path kinks right and left and heads out across a large field with a fence on the left at first, then unfenced across a large field. As you approach Charlton, the line of the path is marked with wooden posts. Join a lane and turn left back to the start, a few yards away.

Fox and Hounds, Singleton.

Walk 6
CHILGROVE AND EAST MARDEN

The Royal Oak, Hooksway

Walk 6

CHILGROVE AND EAST MARDEN

Distance:	4¹/₂ miles
Route:	Chilgrove - Philliswood Lane - Hooksway (optional detour) - East Marden - Hillbarn - Bow Hill Farm - Chilgrove Hill - Chilgrove.
Map:	OS Explorer 120: Chichester
Start/Parking:	At Chilgrove on the B2141 Chichester-to-Harting road. There is room to park on the village green in front of the White Horse pub at GR 828145. Avoid the spaces reserved for pub patrons.
Public Transport:	None convenient
Conditions:	Generally easy walking along good tracks, field paths and across open downland.
Refreshments:	White Horse pub at Chilgrove, Royal Oak at Hooksway (a short distance off the main route).

This is a short but varied walk across undulating countryside deep within the rolling dip slope of the Downs to the north of Chichester. It starts along the quiet valley between Chilgrove and Hooksway, where a short optional detour allows a visit to the Royal Oak, a quintessential downland pub. A short climb out of the valley and a steady descent across fields brings us to the charming village of East Marden. Another short sharp climb up on to Chilgrove Hill is followed by a beautiful open ridge walk with fine views. For more energetic walkers, this walk can be linked with Walk 17 at East Marden or Walk 12 at Hooksway.

THE WALK

Return to the main road **(1)** *and turn right beside it. After a little over 100 yards go right over a stile and follow the direction of a finger post along the right edge of pasture, very gradually diverging from the road to your left. Go over a stile, across a field to a second stile, over a drive and forward along the right edge of two fields. Join a track signposted as a bridleway and bear right to follow it along the floor of a quiet valley. A few yards after passing under power lines fork right and shortly, where the track divides again, keep left (virtually straight on). A track continues within the left edge of pleasant woodland. After about a quarter of a mile, at a way post* **(2),** *turn left through a belt of scrub.*

If in need of refreshment, continue along the valley from this point to reach the Royal Oak at Hooksway, a delightful pub, beautifully set, tucked down in this secluded downland valley. From the pub you can then follow the access lane up to rejoin the walk at point 3. If you would like to extend the walk, the pub is also a link point with Walk 12.

On the direct route from point 2, go half right across pasture and uphill, soon bearing right to walk obliquely up through a rather sparse plantation of young trees. Leave the plantation over a stile and continue with a post and rail fence on your left to join the lane up from the pub **(3).**

Turn left out to the B2141 and left again beside this busy road. Luckily there is a wide grass verge on the right. After about 200 yards go right over a stile beside a gate and ahead across a field to the next stile, in sight. A path, which is normally preserved through any growing crop, heads squarely out across the field beyond. Go straight across a hedged track, using two stiles, and forward across the next field beside a fence and, subsequently, a belt of trees on your right, dropping gently down. In the field corner go ahead over a stile, across a meadow to a second stile and out to a lane where you should turn right into East Marden. After a few yards, opposite a post box on the right **(4),** *the walk continues along a track to the left.*

Allow time to visit the church, only a few yards ahead along the lane and

not to be missed. The building, on raised ground facing the village green, dates from the 13th century and, opposite, stands the old village wellhead and pump, shaded by a circular thatched roof. Return the same way to resume the walk along the track from point 4.

Where the track divides, keep left (almost straight on), soon following it round to the left past farm buildings. Beyond the last barn on your right, go ahead over a stile and along a wide fenced track. Where the enclosed path ends, go forward along a left field edge, dropping down into a dip where a path winds ahead through an area of scrub to a stile. Once over the stile, bear half right, climbing steeply up a grassy slope, to a stile which comes into sight as you approach the top of the hill. An enclosed path continues along the edge of a copse to join a drive where you should turn left.

After about 200 yards (5) turn right along a gravel access drive and, after a little over 100 yards, go left over a stile and forward along a right field edge with a fine view to the left across the valley back to East Marden and beyond. Go through a gate, over a stile and along a path which skirts to the right of the buildings at Bow Hill Farm. Join a concrete drive through a bridle gate and go ahead along it. Pass to the right of a bungalow, go through a gate and ahead along the ridge of Chilgrove Hill, keeping a fence on your right.

This is a fine stretch with good views all the way, northwards across the undulating, well wooded dip slope of the Downs, rising gradually towards the northern edge of the Downs which forms much of the skyline.

Take a straight course through several fields, skirting to the left of an isolated tree clump and continuing to join a track through a bridle gate (6). Turn left and follow this track downhill for less than half a mile, back to the start.

Hooksway from path between points 2 and 3.

Walk 7

DEVIL'S DYKE, EDBURTON HILL AND POYNINGS

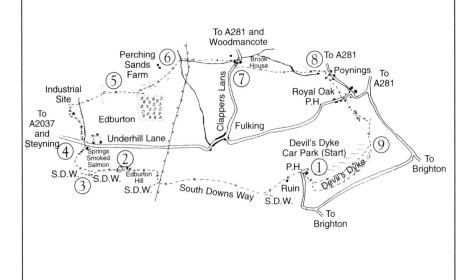

Walk 7

DEVIL'S DYKE, EDBURTON HILL AND POYNINGS

Distance:	6¼ miles
Route:	Devil's Dyke Hotel - South Downs Way - Edburton Hill - Edburton - Perching Sands - Brook House - Poynings - Devil's Dyke - Devil's Dyke Hotel.
Map:	OS Explorer 122: South Downs Way - Steyning to Newhaven.
Start/Parking:	In the car park in front of the Devil's Dyke Hotel, approached northwards from the Dyke Road roundabout on the Brighton by-pass. GR 258112.
Public Transport:	None, except for an occasional special summer bus service from Brighton.
Conditions:	Firm chalk and flint tracks at first, then field paths which may be muddy after rain. One well-graded descent and one steady climb.
Refreshments:	Royal Oak pub at Poynings. Devil's Dyke Hotel at start and finish.

From the tourist honey pot of the Devil's Dyke Hotel this varied walk takes us quickly away along one of the finest stretches of the South Downs Way. After a short but worthwhile detour up to the summit of Edburton Hill, an exceptional viewpoint, a steady descent, using a splendid terraced path, takes us down to the little spring line village of Edburton at the foot of the steep northern Downs escarpment. The return route uses field paths, crossing and re-crossing several tiny streams to reach the larger village of Poynings where there is a well-placed pub. The climb back up to the start offers alternative options, either along the floor or up round the side of the spectacular downland combe known as Devil's Dyke.

THE WALK

From the Dyke Hotel **(1)**, *head out generally westwards, over a stile and along the edge of the steep northern downs escarpment, dropping away to the right. Pass about 50 yards to the right of a ruined brick building and contour along the hillside to a gate where you join the South Downs Way and enter the National Trust area of the Fulking Escarpment.*

The view ahead embraces the masts on Truleigh Hill in the foreground, the remains of Chanctonbury Ring in the middle distance and, beyond, on a clear day, the distant hills on the other side of the Arun valley.

Follow the clear path westwards along the top of the scarp slope for over half a mile. Just after passing under power lines, go through a gate and turn right with a fence on your right, following it round to the left and up to the top of Edburton Hill **(2)**. *Skirt to the left of a sparse group of planted trees, barely surviving on this exposed hilltop, go over a stile and forward across the ditch and ramparts of the 'motte and bailey' marked on OS maps. Continue on a flint path along the escarpment edge, now with a fence on your left and the tiny settlement of Edburton, your next objective, tucked away at the foot of the Downs.*

On reaching a gate providing access back on to the South Downs Way **(3)**, *don't go through it. Instead turn sharply back to the right on a path dropping downhill*

Devil's Dyke with Poynings in the background.

between low banks. After 60 yards, turn left on a terraced path which descends round the side of a deep combe.

This is a fine example of the many so-called 'bostal' paths which, for centuries, have carried traffic up and down the escarpment. The old hollow way, in this case, is overgrown and the used path is along the top of the bank beside it.

The path descends through an area of scrubby woodland, down a flight of steps and out via an access drive to join the Underhill lane.

Edburton Church is reached by a short detour to the right, returning the same way. It dates from the 13th Century and contains a lead font, one of only three in Sussex.

Turn left turn along the lane and, after a few yards only (4), go right along the access drive to Browns Meadow. Just short of the entrance to an industrial site the path bears left skirting to the left of the site with the perimeter fence on your right. In the field corner go forward over a footbridge and turn right along the right edge of two fields with another footbridge between them. In the second field corner (5) go left along a cinder track and, after 40 yards, right along a right field edge, walking parallel to the Downs once more, away to your right.

Maintain direction along the right edge of the field beyond, crossing an intermediate footbridge. Cross a stile, track and footbridge in quick succession and then, with the corner of a copse on your right, veer half left across a field where the path is liable to be obliterated by ploughing. Converge on the hedge on your left and seek out a footbridge, hidden in this hedge. Cross a concrete drive and the stile opposite and head out obliquely across a paddock, following the arrow on the stile. Cross another drive and maintain direction across another paddock.

On the other side of the field (6) go over a stile beside a gate, across a culverted stream and forward along a right field edge, passing beneath power lines, with the stream hidden in the trees to your right. Your path continues, never far from the stream, through several neglected pastures and out to join a lane where you should turn right. After about 200 yards (7) turn left over a stile beside a gate and head for another stile in the far left field corner. Continue in the same direction across a large field.

This is a good vantage point from which to enjoy a wide sweep of the Downs. Directly ahead of you is the wooded slope of Newtimber Hill with the smoother profile of Wolstonbury Hill beyond (both explored on Walk 1). Spread out to your right is the downland escarpment between Devil's Dyke and Truleigh Hill, traversed at the start of the walk.

On either side of the field, cross a stile and descend gently to a footbridge over a stream from which a track continues with the stream now on your right. Follow this track which eventually acquires a concrete surface until, about 20 yards short of a lane (8), you turn right along a narrow tarmac path. At a path junction turn right and, where the path opens out, keep left along the edge of two fields out to join the lane at Poynings. The Royal Oak pub is now in sight to the right, but the walk continues to the left.

After a few yards turn right through the yard of a garage and on along a left field edge. After about 150 yards, go left over a stile, across a dam at the head of a pond and right along a right field edge and then an enclosed path. At a path junction turn right along a wider track, muddy in places.

Beyond a gate where there is a National Trust notice, 'Devil's Dyke' **(9)**, you have a choice. You can either keep right and walk along the floor of the Dyke to its upper end or, preferably, fork left on a rising path which climbs along the side of the Dyke.

Both routes give a fine impression of this remarkable rift, perhaps the most spectacular site in the South Downs, a particularly dramatic example of the dry valleys which are such a notable feature of the downland landscape.

If using the higher route, keep right where the path divides and subsequently right again, past a water trough and along the rim of the Dyke, then right once more across the upper end of the Dyke where the two routes rejoin again. From this point a clear rising path takes you through a gate, up over a bank and through the Dyke Hotel car park back to the start.

Devil's Dyke.

The view from Edburton Hill.

The view from Devil's Dyke Hotel.

Walk 8
BEEDING HILL AND SOUTHWICK HILL

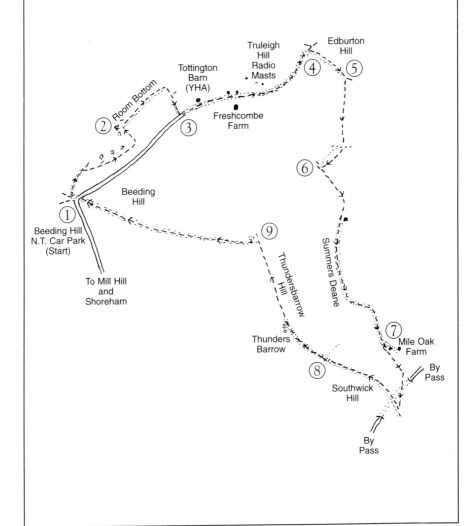

Walk 8

BEEDING HILL AND SOUTHWICK HILL

Distance:	7¹/₂ miles.
Route:	Beeding Hill - Tottington Barn - Truleigh Hill - Edburton Hill - Summers Deane - Southwick Hill - Thundersbarrow Hill - Beeding Hill.
Map:	OS Explorer 122: South Downs Way - Steyning to Newhaven.
Start/Parking:	From the Beeding Hill National Trust car park, to which the only road access is northwards from the Old Shoreham Road about a quarter of a mile east of its junction with the A283. Follow the signs to Mill Hill. Drive past both Mill Hill car parks and continue to reach the NT car park on a bend at GR 208097.
Public Transport:	None convenient unless you start from Mile Oak, joining the walk at point 7.
Conditions:	All along good paths or downland tracks. One well-graded climb.
Refreshments:	None on the route.

This walk explores the rolling, largely treeless, open downland rising gently up the dip slope of the Downs to the north of the urban coastal strip between Hove and Shoreham. Until a few years ago the whole area was something of an arable desert, but much of the land is now under grass, thanks to an expansion of the National Trust holding on Fulking and Edburton Hills and elsewhere, designation as a so-called Environmentally Sensitive Area, a government agri-environmental scheme which encourages reversion to downland pasture. The walk starts out on a fine route along the edge of the steep northern downland escarpment, avoiding at least part of a particularly dreary section of the South

Downs Way, before heading south on an open grassy ridge and then along a quiet valley, almost to the edge of the built up area.

A short climb takes you up on to Southwick Hill, another National Trust area which had a narrow escape from the ravages of the Brighton Bypass. The walk concludes with an airy traverse of Thundersbarrow Hill with spectacular views all the way back to the start.

If you would like a really energetic day out, this walk can be conveniently linked with Walk 7, the link point being point 4, offering 14 miles in all in the form of a figure-of-eight.

THE WALK

Start the walk along a track which leaves the car park to the left of a National Trust notice 'Beeding Hill', past a wooden post in the middle of the track (1) and drops gently downhill between high grassy banks. After about 250 yards, fork right on a path which climbs obliquely up the bank to a kissing gate. After a few more yards, where the path divides, keep right on the higher of the two paths which contours along the hillside with a scrub covered slope dropping away to your left. A path then burrows between areas of scrub as it continues along the rim of a downland combe, bearing gradually left.

At a waypost (2), where the ground begins to drop away in front of you, turn right along the rough grassy hillside, walking parallel to a fence on your right. Shortly, where a sunken track comes up the hill from your left, go ahead through a gate and continue along the side of the hill, walking parallel to a fence on your right.

The downland valley down the hill to your left, Room Bottom, was once quiet and unspoilt, but has now been badly disfigured by the establishment of a motor cycle racing track which, luckily, is only permitted to function on a limited number of days per year.

Where the fence on your right ends, turn squarely right and climb across open downland to join and follow another fence, keeping it on your right. Go through two successive gates out to join the South Downs Way (3) and turn left to follow this gravel track past Tottington Barn, a youth hostel, and on over Truleigh Hill.

This, sadly, is one of the least attractive sections of this long distance route, disfigured by bungalows, derelict sheds, and four radio masts. Let us hope that, under new rights of way legislation, it may be possible to establish a better route, at least for walkers, nearer the edge of the escarpment. Some compensation is available in the form of a superb view southwards to the coastal plain.

After half a mile the South Downs Way drops down into a shallow dip where you will pass to the right of a National Trust notice indicating the start of their Fulking Escarpment open access area. From a gate in the dip **(4)**, the link point with Walk 7, continue with the South Downs Way as it curves right round the right shoulder of Edburton Hill. Now you can walk on the grass, parallel and to the left of the track, much pleasanter underfoot than the hard flinty surface of the main route.

Where the ground levels out **(5)** turn right over a stile in a fence to the right of the South Downs Way and head squarely out along the summit of a grassy ridge with the ground dropping gently away on both sides. There is no defined path but keep to the centre of the ridge, losing height very gradually, and you won't go wrong. Go over a stile in a crossing fence and bear half right, dropping steeply into a valley, reaching the bottom of the hill, a few yards to the left of a bridle gate **(6)**.

Turn left along the floor of the valley but, after a few yards, veer half right up over a grassy shoulder, with the protruding tip of an electricity pylon as a marker ahead. Once over the shoulder you can aim for a partially roofless brick barn. Go through a gate about 60 yards to the right of the barn and follow a substantial track on along the valley (Summers Deane), ignoring a track off to the right.

After a little over a mile, about 100 yards short of the first barn at Mile Oak Farm **(7)**, go right over a stile beside a gate and forward along a track which bears left and climbs obliquely up the hillside. At a National Trust notice 'Southwick Hill' go straight ahead.

View across to Chanctonbury Ring from the path between points 2 and 3, Steyning in middle distance.

This fine open area, a pleasant mixture of chalk downland pasture and patchy gorse and scrub, was only saved from irreparable damage when the Department of Transport was required to construct a bored tunnel beneath it for the Brighton bypass after the cheaper option of a cutting and a short 'cut-and-cover' tunnel was rejected.

At the top of the hill you will come to a stile beside a gate. Don't cross the stile. Instead turn back to the right along the edge of the NT area, walking roughly parallel to a fence on your left. After over a quarter of a mile, about 40 yards short of the point where the fence on your left turns squarely right at the corner of the NT area (8), you should sidestep to the left over a stile and turn right through a bridle gate between two farm gates. Now go ahead along a fenced track which climbs gently to follow the ridge of Thundersbarrow Hill.

Beyond the next gate, you will pass, on your left, two tumuli, the Thunders Barrow which gives the hill its name. It is the site of an Iron Age hill fort and, later, a farm settlement covering more than an acre and occupied from the 1st to the 4th centuries. From here there is a fine panoramic view embracing, clockwise from the coast, the ridge of Steep Down, Cissbury Ring, Chanctonbury Ring, the masts on Truleigh Hill, Edburton Hill, Fulking Hill and the Devil's Dyke hotel and viewpoint.

View towards Tottington Mount from the path above Room Bottom.

Carry on in the same direction across the open summit of *Thundersbarrow Hill*. Just past the next gate, at a waypost **(9)**, turn left, leaving a silage enclosure on your right and follow a fenced path which soon drops down into a valley and straight up the other side. Continue along this clear path over the shoulder of Beeding Hill and back to the start.

From the final, gentle, descent a view opens out ahead along the full length of the lower Adur valley. Towards the mouth of the river at Shoreham you can pick out the old toll crossing and the newer A27 bridge, and straight ahead, the villages of Upper Beeding, Bramber and Steyning with Chanctonbury Ring in the background.

Walk 9
BURPHAM AND BARPHAM HILL

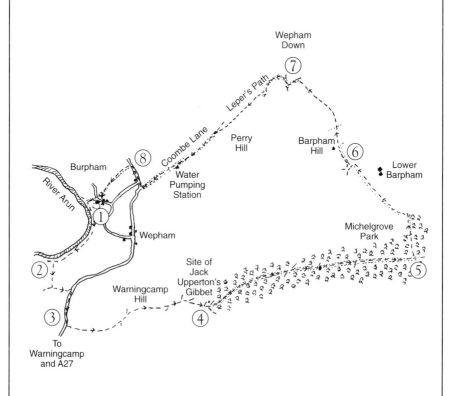

Walk 9

BURPHAM AND BARPHAM HILL

Distance:	7¹/₂ miles.
Route:	Burpham - River Arun - Michelgrove Park - Barpham Hill - Wepham Down - Leper's Path - Coombe Lane - Burpham.
Map:	OS Explorer 121: Arundel and Pulborough.
Start/Parking:	From the village of Burpham, accessible by road only from the A27 east of Arundel Station. Follow a lane via Warningcamp and Wepham and park in Burpham recreation ground car park behind the George and Dragon pub. GR 039088.
Public Transport:	None convenient.
Conditions:	All on excellent paths or tracks
Refreshments:	Pub at Burpham

Within the compass of an easy half-day circuit, this is a remarkably varied walk which manages to sample many of the contrasting landscape features of the West Sussex downland. It starts and finishes at the isolated village of Burpham, once a Saxon fortified township (the name comes from the Old English, *Burh Ham*, meaning 'a settlement by a stronghold'), built by King Alfred to defend the river valley against the Danes and strategically set on a low promontory on the east side of the Arun valley. The walk quickly drops down to follow the river for the best part of a mile downstream with fine views towards Arundel Castle before burrowing into the Downs along the floor of a secluded dry valley.

A less interesting mile through dense beech wood to Michelgrove follows but the best of the walk is still ahead. Emerging with some relief from the trees, we traverse along the upper slope of another delightful combe, using one of my favourite paths, to reach the high open downland of Barpham Hill with superb views in all directions. A terraced path slants down to join and follow an old lane, now a shady track, back towards Burpham which is finally reached along a field path and past the church, parts of which date back to the 13th century.

THE WALK

From the car park **(1),** *return to the lane by the George and Dragon pub, turn left and, after a few yards, go forward along a No Through Road which soon dwindles to a path. Where it divides, fork left. The path descends to follow the foot of a scrub covered slope. After about 350 yards go right over a stile and ahead along a raised bank parallel to a redundant loop of the River Arun, hidden behind reed beds on your right.*

From this path you get a good view ahead along the Arun valley to Arundel Castle and, across the valley to your right, the heights of Arundel Park where you can pick out a descending path used on Walk 3.

After almost half a mile **(2),** *at a waypost sandwiched between two stiles, turn left down a bank to a third stile and go forward along a wide green strip between drainage ditches. Continue with a hedge and ditch on your left to reach another stile, beyond which you should turn left along a grassy path, still with a ditch on your left.*

Lower Barpham.

Distant view towards Chanctonbury Ring from path beyond point 4.

Beyond another stile a track continues out to a lane where you should turn sharply back to the right.

After about a quarter of a mile **(3)** turn left through a gap in wooden railings and along a path signed as a bridleway which contours along near the foot of a wooded slope to a gate and then along the floor of a secluded downland combe, where you should ignore paths to right and left. At a junction with a more substantial track turn left. After 100 yards, at a Y-junction, fork right, and, after another 30 yards, fork right again, to climb through woodland. Towards the top of the hill, go straight over a crossing track and, after a few more yards, join a tarmac forestry road and turn left.

After a few yards, at a way post, make a detour along a narrow path into the wood on your left to seek out a wooden plaque on which is carved the image of a gibbet and the inscription 'JU 1774', marking the spot where Jack Upperton, a notorious highwayman, was hanged at the scene of his crime, once part of an old road over the downs.

From the waypost **(4)**, go ahead along the main metalled forestry road and follow it between beech woods for three quarters of a mile, ignoring all side turnings. Pass to the left of an isolated house and go forward, now on a roughly metalled track, once again ignoring side paths. Continue for more than half a mile until, at a Y-junction **(5)**, you should fork left. Shortly go ahead through a woodland clearing and on along a rutted track which, after leaving the wood, continues along a right field edge before *traversing along the upper slope of a lovely downland valley.*

Views soon open out to the right across a wide expanse of rolling downland with the domed Harrow Hill prominent in the foreground and, to the right of it, a glimpse of the battered remains of Chanctonbury Ring. Tucked down at the foot of the slope is the picturesque farm complex at Lower Barpham.

Beyond a gate (6), the track bears round to the left to reach an isolated waypost where you should turn sharply back to the right now on a chalk and flint track. Go through a bridle gate to the right of a double farm gate, and ahead along a track which runs parallel to a fence on your right and continues across the top of Barpham Hill, passing about 50 yards to the right of the trig point on the 468 ft summit. Where the track ends in the middle of the field, go ahead in the same direction to a gate, in sight.

From this path a fine panorama opens out to the left towards Arundel and the sea, with a long stretch of the western Downs between Arundel Park (Walk 3) and Duncton Hill (Walk 10).

Carry on along the open grassy ridge before dropping down to join a track through a gate, where you should turn left. After about 100 yards, at a junction (7), follow the concrete-surfaced track round to the right and, after 20 yards, fork left along another clear track which curves steadily round to the left and heads for the sea, along the upper slope of Perry Hill. Shortly, fork right along a signed footpath which drops obliquely down across a field to a stile, with the village of Burpham, half hidden by trees, directly ahead.

This fine terraced track is known locally as the Leper's Path because it once formed part of a link between a leper colony on the site of the present day Angmering Lea Farm and the chapel of St James which stood near Offham (Walk 2) until the 15th century.

Beyond a stile, a shallow terraced path continues down the grassy slope. At the bottom of the hill join and go forward along a hedged track which becomes the drive from a water pumping station and takes you along the valley to join a road. Turn right and shortly where the road to Burpham bears left, fork right (almost directly ahead) along a narrower lane. After another 200 yards (8) go left along a footpath which follows a left field edge. Go over a low wall into Burpham churchyard, walk anti-clockwise round behind the church, past the church porch and out to the lane opposite the George and Dragon pub.

Burpham Church.

The walk up the valley beyond point 3.

Walk 10
BIGNOR POST, SUTTON AND DUNCTON

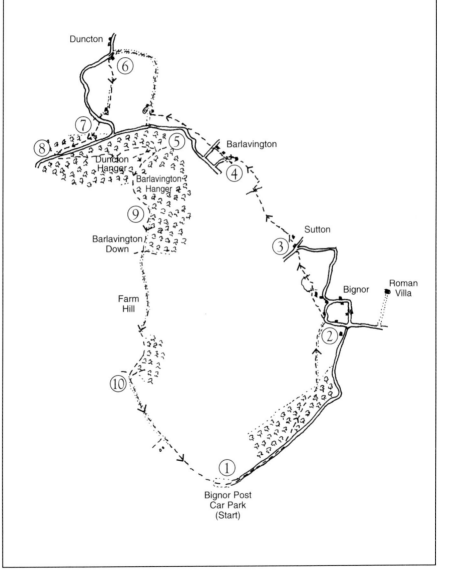

Duncton

⑥

⑦

⑧

⑤

Barlavington

Duncton Hanger

Barlavington Hanger

④

⑨

Barlavington Down

③

Sutton

Bignor

Roman Villa

Farm Hill

②

⑩

①

Bignor Post
Car Park
(Start)

Walk 10
BIGNOR POST, SUTTON AND DUNCTON

Distance:	7³/₄ miles
Route:	Bignor Post - Bignor - Sutton - Barlavington - Duncton - Duncton Hanger - Barlavington Down - Bignor Post.
Map:	OS Explorer 121: Arundel and Pulborough.
Start/Parking:	From Bignor Post, which is reached from the underhill lane at Bignor along a rather uneven unsigned lane which climbs to the top of the Downs where you can park in the National Trust car park at GR 974129.
Public Transport:	None convenient
Conditions:	Much of the walk follows clear well-used paths and tracks. One well-graded climb up through Duncton Hanger and on to Bignor Hill.
Refreshments:	Pubs at Sutton and Duncton

Starting from one of the highest points on the downs at Bignor Post, this walk quickly drops down the wooded northern slope of the Downs to explore the gently undulating downland foothills where water bubbles up from beneath the chalk to flow northwards and a series of so-called 'spring line' villages have developed over the centuries. At Bignor, path and stream share the same route for a short distance. Approaching Sutton, the path winds through a sheltered valley, crossing and re-crossing the stream and at Duncton the water has been dammed to form a large pond on the site of a disused flour mill, now converted to fish ponds.

The return route climbs steadily up through Duncton Hanger to a superb viewpoint on Duncton Hill and then traverses along the escarpment, past Farm Hill, an excellent place for chalk downland wild flowers. A final ascent across more open downland brings us back to the start.

THE WALK

From the car park (1) start out by walking back down the access road by which you reached the car park. After a little over a quarter of a mile, fork left along a narrow path which drops obliquely down the wooded slope. Towards the bottom, join a track coming in from your left and, after a few yards, go left to leave the wood and follow a path, enclosed between fence and woodland, then along a track, partly shared with a tiny stream, to join a lane at Bignor (2).

A right turn here takes you to Bignor Roman Villa, about a quarter of a mile off the route, on the line of Stane Street, the Roman route between London and Chichester. The villa contains some of the best preserved mosaic floors in the country, including one 80ft long. One area has been excavated to give a good demonstration of the way the Roman hypocaust heating system functioned. There is a shop and tea room and the villa is open from March to October from 10 to 5. Return the same way.

From point 2, turn left and, after 100 yards, fork left through a wicket gate, go forward along the foot of a grassy bank and on through a quiet wooded valley crossing and re-crossing a stream. Leave the wood over a stile by a gate and head squarely out across two fields, climbing gently to a stile, from which a grassy strip continues, unfenced, between two fields, and on along a short enclosed path to join the lane at

Barlavington Church and farm.

Sutton opposite the White Horse pub **(3)**.

Go forward for a few yards past the pub, and then turn left along the right edge of the access to the pub car park to enter an enclosed path. Where this path ends, go right through a gate, left and right past a shed and ahead across a lawn to another gate. A defined track now bears half left across a large field. On the other side of the field go straight on, dropping down along

Bignor Post.

the right edge of rough pasture, ignoring signed paths to left and right. A path then winds down through a wood to cross a stream. Now bear half right up across a sloping meadow to cross a stile and turn left uphill along a left field edge and then forward along a fenced grass track. At a junction with a farm track, turn left and follow it as it skirts to the left of the farm buildings to enter Barlavington churchyard **(4)**.

The simple 13th century church is beautifully set, surrounded by trees and next to a working farm. In the churchyard are two seats carved from massive tree trunks, one of them nicely placed beside the churchyard wall with a fine view southwards towards the steep wooded downs escarpment.

Leave the churchyard and turn left along the lane from the church. Where it bends left, fork right along a gravel access drive and, where this ends, go ahead along a hedged path which soon drops down to cross a stream and a lane. Go up the steps opposite and along a headland path. Where the hedge on your left turns away to the right, go forward across a field to reach a lane **(5)**.

Don't join the lane. Instead, bear right along a wide track, signed as a bridleway. Ignoring another signed bridleway to the right, go ahead on a path within the left edge of woodland and past a neglected orchard to join a tarmac drive. Turn right past Duncton Mill Pond.

Once a corn mill, the sandstone mill house and associated buildings are now incorporated into a fish farm.

Shortly go forward along a gravel track, ignoring another track off to the right.

Continue with this track which bears left to become a metalled drive once more and takes you out to the A285 south of Duncton. Turn left to walk along a loop of old road, passing in front of the Cricketers Inn **(6)**.
The Cricketers acquired its present name in 1860 when John Wisden, of Almanac fame, took it over. The figure on the inn sign is of James Dean who played for Sussex and England in the 19th century.

The path across Farm Hill.

At the point where the old road rejoins the main A285, turn left along a narrow path which squeezes to the right of the pub garden, winds through a wooded dip to a stream crossing and stile and continues between fences across a field to a stile, gently uphill along a right field edge and on past a farm on your right. Soon after a high wall on your right ends, go right and left out to the A285 **(7)**.

Cross the road, go through a gap in the hedge opposite and straight out across a field to enter woodland at the foot of the steep downland escarpment. A footpath continues obliquely right to climb steadily up through the wood. After about a quarter of a mile, at a signpost, go sharply back to the left out to reach a small parking area **(8)** with a fine view overlooking Duncton and the Weald.

From the entrance to the car park cross the road to enter a track past a wooden pole barrier, immediately veering left on a terraced path along the wooded hill side, at first walking parallel to the road, down the hill to your left, passing a notice indicating that you are entering Duncton Hanger, a designated Site of Special Scientific Interest. Join and follow a signed bridleway coming up the hill from behind on your left and follow it as it contours along the hanger.

After the best part of half a mile, at a junction of several paths, turn sharply back to the right, now climbing. At a 3-arm sign, turn left, now on a level path and, after about 100 yards, at a T-junction, turn right to climb once more. The path finally *emerges to level out as it continues along the top edge of the hanger to reach a fine viewpoint (9).*

From a well-placed seat an exceptional view unfolds ahead along the line of the Downs. On a clear day you should be able to pick out the distant promontory of Wolstonbury Hill, 20 miles away.

The path drops steeply down a grassy hillside and continues as a tree lined path across a dip. Go straight over a crossing track and ahead on a wide unfenced grassy strip between two large fields. Beyond a bridle gate an enclosed track continues along the flank of Farm Hill, a good spot for chalk downland wild flowers in the spring and early summer. A fenced path crosses another shallow dip in the downland. At a meeting of several paths (10), go ahead for 10 yards and then fork left across a corner to join and follow a wide chalk and flint track steadily uphill. At the top, continue with the track as it passes well to the left of two prominent radio masts, and on for another quarter of a mile back to the start.

The area around Bignor Post is part of the 3500 acre Slindon Estate, in the hands of the National Trust since 1950. The immediate area round the post is available as an open access area, but on much of the estate you are restricted to public rights of way across farmland.

Duncton Mill pond.

Walk 11
THE TRUNDLE, WEST DEAN
AND SINGLETON

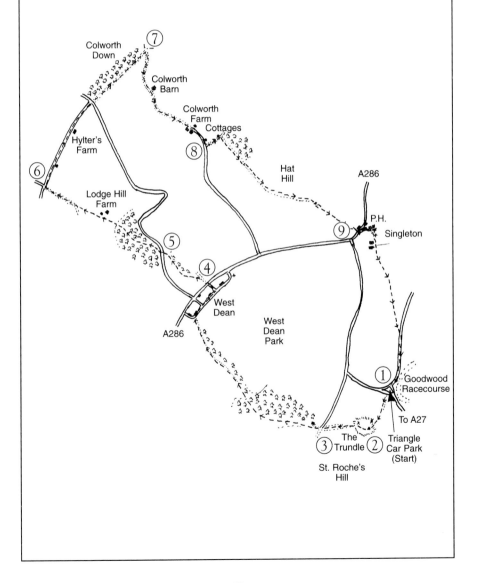

Walk 11

THE TRUNDLE, WEST DEAN AND SINGLETON

Distance:	8 miles
Route:	Goodwood Country Park - The Trundle - West Dean - Hylter's Farm - Colworth Down - Colworth Farm - Hat Hill - Singleton - Goodwood Country Park.
Map:	OS Explorer 120: Chichester
Start/Parking:	Follow signs to Goodwood Racecourse from the roundabout on the A27 at the eastern end of the Chichester bypass. Pass to the left of the main racecourse buildings and park in the Triangle car park at GR 879113.
Public Transport:	None
Conditions:	A pleasant mix of chalk and flint tracks and short stretches over open grass downland. Half a mile of quiet lane.
Refreshments:	Pub at West Dean (just off the walk route) and at Singleton.

Starting high on the Downs, this walk begins with a short sharp climb up to the open grassy summit of St Roche's Hill, part of the Goodwood Country Park and crowned by the ramparts of an Iron Age Fort known as The Trundle (from the Anglo-Saxon 'tryndel', meaning a circle). A steady descent then brings us down to the village of West Dean in the valley formed by the River Lavant, normally dry during the summer months but transformed during recent wet winters into an overflowing torrent. An undulating route then follows good tracks and paths northwards and eastwards across the rolling dip slope of the Downs, much of it within the West Dean Estate where there are plenty of notices informing you where you can't walk and rather fewer telling you where you can go! The walk, all on rights of way, rises in stages to Hat Hill, a fine viewpoint, from which a steep descent leads down into the charming flint village of Singleton where the Fox and Hounds pub provides a warm welcome for walkers. Suitably refreshed you will make short work of the steady but not unduly steep one-mile climb back up to the start.

A short car journey from the start of the walk is the Weald and Downland Museum, a remarkable collection of historical buildings which have been saved from demolition and painstakingly dismantled and re-erected on a large open air site.

THE WALK

From the car park (1) cross the road on the northern side of the triangle of roads surrounding the parking area and start out up a grassy slope to the right of a flight of wide steps, passing a notice describing features of the view back to the north.

This view is indeed a fine one across a wide prospect of rolling well-wooded downland rising in undulating stages to the heights of the northern escarpment on the distant skyline. In the foreground are Levin Down (Walk 5), Singleton village and Hat Hill, crossed on the return route of the present walk.

River Lavant in flood at West Dean.

Go through a swing gate and climb beside a fence, continuing through the ramparts of The Trundle and up to the trig point on the 677 ft summit of St Roche's Hill (2). From this point, once the site of a medieval chapel, now long gone, dedicated to St. Roch, another exceptional view opens out to the south over a wide panorama of the coastal plain between Worthing and Portsmouth with the spire of Chichester Cathedral providing a prominent landmark. The Isle of Wight is visible to the southwest.

At the trig point turn right and join a track immediately to the left of the second of the two radio masts which disfigure the summit. Follow this clear track through a swing gate and westwards for a quarter of a mile to join a lane just past the Seven Points car park (3). Cross the road and follow a path opposite which starts to the left of a gravel access drive to a rather grand, recently restored house.

After 100 yards, where the path divides, keep right, soon entering woodland. The track through the wood eventually comes out into the open to follow a flint wall surrounding the grounds of West Dean Park down into a valley. At the bottom of the hill, cross a brick bridge over the River Lavant, a winterbourne which may, depending on the season and the weather, be anything from a parched ditch to a wide stream. Join and bear right along a lane.

West Dean Gardens, nearby, are open daily from March to October and incorporate ornamental and kitchen gardens, a 250 acre landscaped park and a

The route near point 7.

50 acre arboretum, linked by a 2¼ mile walk.

*After about 300 yards along the lane, with the Lavant on your right, take the second turning on the left, just past a cottage with a date label '1995' on it and walk up to join the A286 **(4)**.*

*Cross the road and follow the track opposite. After about 150 yards, at a waypost, fork left along a narrow path which contours along at the foot of a wooded slope rising up on your right for a quarter of a mile before bearing left across a shallow grassy dip to join a road **(5)**. Go right for 15 yards and then fork left along a wide woodland path which gradually gains height.*

Leave the wood over a stile and go ahead, soon crossing two stiles as you skirt to the left of the substantial farm house and outbuildings of Lodge Hill Farm, then veer slightly left down across a field to another stile, in sight. Head squarely out across the next two fields, dropping down to join a track. Maintain direction along this track as it climbs ahead out of the valley.

*On reaching a lane **(6)** turn right. After about two thirds of a mile, at a road junction, go straight ahead through a gate and along a wide unmade track with woodland on your left. After almost half a mile where the track widens out and several ways meet **(7)**, turn sharply back to the right along a headland track with a hedge on your left, dropping gently downhill to pass a large, currently deserted, flint farm house in a dip before climbing again. Beyond the buildings at Colworth Farm, the track becomes a metalled lane.*

*Go forward along this lane for about 150 yards until, just past a linked pair of isolated cottages, improbably numbered 142 and 143 **(8)**, you should turn left along a roughly metalled track. Immediately beyond a derelict Nissan hut on your left, turn right up a bank and forward along a left field edge until you can sidestep to the left over a stile in the hedge and go right, resuming your previous direction, now along the right edge of three fields, over Hat Hill and then downhill.*

A fine view opens up ahead across the valley ahead to Levin Down (Walk 5) with Singleton tucked down in the foreground and, beyond the village, a long valley stretching away towards Charlton and East Dean (Walk 16). Over to the right the ugly modern grandstand at Goodwood racecourse strikes a jarring note, while nearer at hand, half hidden by trees, also to your right, you can catch a glimpse of the complex of old buildings which make up the Weald and Downland Open Air Museum.

*Drop down, keeping close to the fence on your right and crossing two stiles in intermediate crossing fences. Descend a flight of concrete steps, go forward across a brick bridge over the old Midhurst-to-Chichester railway, now disused, and follow a clear path, hedged at first. Go right and left, signed and stiled, to continue alongside the Lavant stream along the left edge of a cricket ground and out to the A286 **(9)**. Go left and, after a few yards, fork right along a lane through Singleton village.*

Colworth Barn.

Singleton is a characteristic downland village, largely flint-built. The church has a Saxon tower and nave, medieval stained glass and a minstrels' gallery.

Just short of the Fox and Hounds pub on the left, turn right along a narrow lane to the church. Go through a gate into the churchyard and immediately turn right, signposted to The Trundle, to follow a flint wall along the edge of the churchyard to a gate. Now go forward, passing to the left of several barns and climb steadily on a clear path, punctuated by stiles. Where the fence on your left ends, go ahead across a field where the path is marked by wooden posts. Join a lane and bear right back to the start. There is a good grass verge for most of the way.

Walk 12
HARTING DOWNS, BEACON HILL AND HOOKSWAY

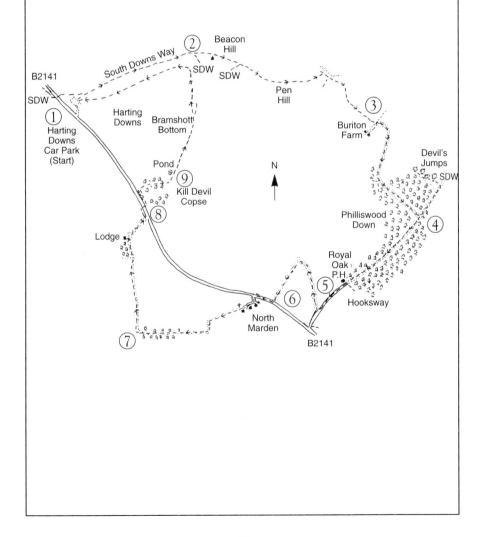

Walk 12

HARTING DOWNS, BEACON HILL AND HOOKSWAY

Distance:	8 miles
Route:	Harting Downs - Beacon Hill - Pen Hill - Buriton Farm - Devil's Jumps - Hooksway - North Marden - Kill Devil Copse - Bramshott Bottom - Harting Downs.
Map:	OS Explorer 120: Chichester
Start/Parking:	At the Harting Downs National Trust Car Park, signposted to the east of the B2141 Chichester-to-South Harting road about a mile south of South Harting at the summit of the Downs. GR 790180
Public Transport:	None
Conditions:	A fairly strenuous up and down walk across open downland and on good tracks and paths.
Refreshments:	Royal Oak pub at Hooksway.

This exceptional walk begins and ends on the top of Harting Downs, a 550-acre area of chalk grass downland and patchy scrub, owned and managed by the National Trust and to which the public are permitted free open access. Starting out along one of the finest open stretches of the South Downs Way, it follows a fairly strenuous switchback route over the summits of Beacon Hill and Pen Hill on the northern escarpment of the Downs. After heading south through woodland, a short detour allows a visit to the striking row of Bronze Age barrows known as the Devil's Jumps. A steady descent brings us down to the tiny secluded hamlet of Hooksway with its welcome pub. Another short climb up to North Marden is rewarded by a chance to visit the tiny flint-built church. On the return route, back within the National Trust open access area, we can enjoy a delightful walk, gently up along the floor of the sheltered downland combe of Bramshott Bottom.

North Marden Church.

THE WALK

From the car park (1) start the walk eastwards along the South Downs Way which keeps close to the edge of the escarpment, with the ground dropping steeply away to your left. After a little over half a mile the path drops down to reach a solid oak waypost at the northern end of Bramshott Bottom (2). Go straight ahead here, climbing steeply to the trig point on the summit of Beacon Hill.

From here, assisted by a helpful direction indicator plate, you can pick out from the wide Wealden panorama to the north, the distant summit of Blackdown, the highest point in Sussex and, in the middle foreground the more modest hillocks of Older Hill and Telegraph Hill. The summit is crowned by traces of an Iron Age hill fort.

Continue down into the next dip and sharply up on to Pen Hill, then down again once more with a fine view ahead along the line of the Downs. Treyford Hill is the prominent bump in the foreground. On reaching a belt of trees turn right, still with the South Downs Way, keeping the trees and a parallel track on your left. The path curves to the right along the lower edge of a large field, soon bearing left within the right edge of an area of scrubby woodland. Ignore a path downhill to the left and head out on a fenced track between two large fields.

At a T-junction with a farm track **(3)** turn left and, after 30 yards, right on a track which soon climbs obliquely up out of the valley. After a little over half a mile, at a T-junction, where the South Downs Way goes off to the left **(4)**, you should turn right.

A short detour to the left from this point, continuing along the South Downs Way, brings you to the Devil's Jumps, accessible via a narrow path to the left of the track. This striking row of Bronze Age Barrows, covered in thick scrub until about 20 years ago, are now kept clear under the management of the Murray Downland Trust who also look after Heyshott Down (Walk 4). Return the same way to point 4.

Follow a wide track steadily downhill for a little over half a mile to reach Hooksway where you can go forward past the Royal Oak inn **(5)**, *occupying a delightfully secluded site, tucked down in a quiet downland valley. Climb ahead along the access lane until, about two thirds of the way up the hill, you can turn sharply back to the right along a roughly made up track, signed as a bridleway. After about 600 yards, at a signed junction, turn left and follow a narrower enclosed path out to join the B2141 road* **(6)**.

Cross the road and turn right along the wide grass verge until, after about 150 yards, you can go left along the lane to North Marden. Very shortly go right along the drive to Church Farm. Follow the drive passing North Marden Church on your right.

Devil's Jumps.

69

This simple, completely unspoilt, church, much of which dates from the 12th century, consists of a single room with an unusual semi-circular or 'apsidal' recess at its eastern end.

Where the drive ends, go ahead along a short enclosed path and on downhill along a right field edge. At the bottom of the hill go forward and left round two sides of a young tree plantation, then right and gently uphill along a right field edge. Beyond the field corner a path continues, soon within a wooded strip. Where this path ends at a stile and you have a choice of three signed paths (7), turn right along a right field edge, soon following this field boundary as it curves round to the right and heads north.

At the end of the field go ahead along a path which skirts along the right hand edge of a copse, passing a lodge with an attached brick archway.

This was once an access point to the Uppark estate, which covers a large area to which there is, deplorably, no public access on foot. The 17th Century mansion at Uppark was destroyed by fire in 1989 but has been painstakingly restored by the National Trust and is open to the public between April and October daily except Friday and Saturday. Access by car is from the B2146 about 1½ miles south of South Harting.

Continue along a clear track from the lodge. Just short of the B2141 turn left along a path running parallel to the road and, after about 60 yards, turn right across the road and follow the track opposite (8). After 30 yards turn left along a fenced path which heads generally north, parallel to the B2141 but well insulated from it by a strip

Harting Downs.

of woodland. After a little over 200 yards go right through a swing gate and ahead on a clear path through a coppice, ignoring all side paths. Beyond staggered railings the path drops down through a patchy yew thicket. At the bottom of the hill the path opens out into a delightful downland valley, Bramshott Bottom, a delectable spot **(9)**. Bear left

Beacon Hill from Harting Downs.

and follow a grassy path gently up along the floor of this valley.

The whole area between here and the end of the walk is managed by the National Trust and is a public access area. The Trust have embarked on an extensive programme of scrub clearance along the sides of Bramshott Bottom, the aim being to restore additional areas of chalk grass downland.

About half way up this downland combe keep left on a path which runs along the left side of the valley, gradually gaining height As you approach the northern end of the combe turn left through a bridle gate and climb up on to Harting Downs, continuing across open downland, walking parallel to your outgoing route, back to the start.

The path back up to Harting Downs.

Walk 13
COOMBES AND CISSBURY RING

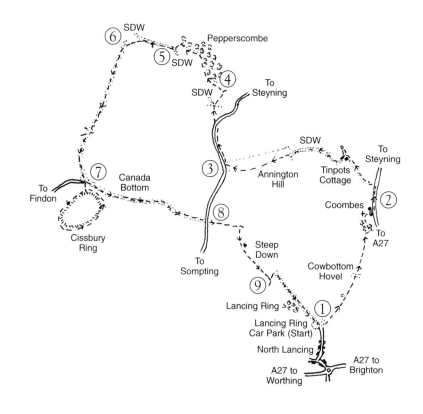

Walk 13

COOMBES AND CISSBURY RING

Distance:	12¹/₂ miles (including circuit of Cissbury Ring)
Route:	Lancing Ring - Coombes - Annington Hill - Pepperscombe - Stump Barn - Cissbury Ring - Steep Down - Lancing Ring
Map:	OS Explorer 122: South Downs Way - Steyning to Newhaven and OS Explorer 121 - Arundel and Pulborough.
Start/Parking:	From the roundabout on the A27 at North Lancing, follow Manor Road northwards, then turn right along Mill Road and follow it to the Lancing Ring car park at GR 182062 where the walk starts.
Public Transport:	Bus to North Lancing
Conditions:	Much of the walk is along good downland tracks or paths. One stretch of open grass downland on Annington Hill. Several climbs, none long or severe.
Refreshments:	None

This is an exhilarating walk, mostly across high rolling downland. It starts from the edge of the built-up coastal conurbation about half way between Brighton and Worthing but is quickly away across undulating hills on the western side of the Adur valley, before descending briefly to visit the tiny hamlet of Coombes with its delightful isolated church. It then joins the South Downs Way for a steady climb up on to the open pastures of Annington Hill. After skirting round the head of the wooded Pepperscombe with views northwards across the Weald, we head south to visit two notable summits overlooking the coastal plain. The circuit of Cissbury Ring is the highlight of the walk and the return route also diverts up and along the ridge of Steep Down, another exceptional viewpoint.

THE WALK

Walk back to the car park entrance **(1),** *cross the access road and go ahead along a grassy path, opposite. At a gravel track turn right and, after 50 yards go left over a stile. Cross a shallow dip to a second stile and continue across a large field where a path should be trodden out through any growing crop. On the other side of the field, go over a third stile and follow a fenced path which drops down into a valley, passing to the right of a substantial flint-walled enclosure (Cowbottom Hovel).*

Climb again on a clear fenced track. Cross a concrete farm track, go through the gate opposite and on along a grassy fenced path. At a field corner turn right. Ignore the first bridle gate on your left and, after a few more yards, go left through a second bridle gate and downhill on a path though woodland which brings you out next to Coombes Church.

Delightfully situated on the lower slopes of the combe, the church is a simple structure of Saxon origins with flint walls, a roof of Horsham stone and a tiny red-tiled belfry. Inside are some wall paintings dating from the 12th century. The village of Coombes, mentioned in the Domesday Book, now consists of little more than the church, farm and a handful of cottages.

From the church continue down through a paddock and out past Coombes Farm to

Cissbury Ring.

join a lane (2). Turn left. After a little over a quarter of a mile, when standing beneath power lines, go left on a signed bridleway which drops down a scrub-covered bank to a gate and then climbs steadily along a left field edge, passing a white walled cottage on your left.

This is Tinpots Cottage. The unusual name may be derived from the fact that it lies on the ancient route by which tin was carried from Cornwall to the port of Pevensey in East Sussex.

Shortly beyond the cottage, go left through a bridle gate and climb to join a track where you should turn left, doubling back on your previous direction, now on part of the South Downs Way. Follow the track as it climbs steadily for over a mile on to Annington Hill. Once out on to open downland go directly ahead up the ridge. At the top of the hill (3) go through a gate in the top right field corner and follow a track which runs parallel and to the right of the Steyning Bostal road.

Across the valley to the left there is a good view of the ramparts of Cissbury Ring which you will be visiting later on the walk.

In the next field corner go through a gate and forward, still on a segregated path to the right of the road. After a little over 100 yards, follow the South Downs Way as it crosses the road and veers half right along an unfenced tarmac track. On the far side of the field, go over a crossing track and immediately, where the South Downs Way goes ahead, you should fork right on a clear path signed as a bridleway to Steyning. The path skirts along the right hand edge of an area of scrub and rough pasture with a fence, right.

As the path crosses a summit, a fine panoramic view of the Weald opens out ahead. Away to your right along the line of the Downs escarpment you can pick out the masts on Truleigh Hill and beyond, the overlapping profiles of Newtimber Hill and Wolstonbury Hill (Walk 1).

The path descends to a T-junction (4) where there is a well-placed memorial seat. Turn left here on a path which follows the rim of Pepperscombe with a wooded slope dropping away to your right. After about a quarter of a mile, fork left on the higher of two paths. After another 300 yards or so the path bears left and climbs beside a fence, right, to rejoin the South Downs Way (5). Turn right.

After another quarter of a mile, where the track divides, fork left, parting company with the South Downs Way once more. At a T-junction, at a point marked as Stump Barn on OS maps, though the barn has disappeared, turn left (6). Follow a wide track generally southwards for well over a mile, ignoring all side and crossing tracks, with your next objective, Cissbury Ring, in sight ahead. Just past a small car park where the lane from Findon comes up from the right (7), the main walk continues to the left.

Allow time, if possible, to go ahead up on to Cissbury Ring, for a circular tour of the ramparts, adding a little over a mile to the walk. Cissbury Ring is the largest and most spectacular prehistoric site on the South Downs. Originally the site of Neolithic flint mines, it became an Iron Age fort and a Roman farm before being refortified to repel Saxon invaders. On a clear day the views along the coastal plain extend from Beachy Head to the Isle of Wight. It is now preserved as an important area of unspoilt chalk downland.

*Having returned to point 7, follow a clear chalk and flint track eastwards, dropping gently into a downland valley, Canada Bottom, once again ignoring all side paths and tracks. Climb again where you have a choice of two parallel tracks (either will do). Cross the Steyning-Sompting road **(8)** and follow the clear track ahead. Ignore the first waymarked bridleway to the right. At a meeting of four paths, just short of a gate, fork right and after a few yards, with an electricity pylon on your left, fork right again on a grassy path which soon climbs steeply up on to Steep Down, past a trig point on the summit and on along a ridge.*

*At the far end of the ridge, drop down to a crossing track **(9),** where you should turn sharply back to the left. After less than 100 yards, turn sharply right on a clear track which skirts to the left of a tree clump, Lancing Ring, on the next hill and takes you back to the start.*

The area around the Ring is managed as a Local Nature Reserve and is also a public open access area. It offers a mixture of chalk grassland, woodland and scrub, embracing a variety of wild life habitats. There is also a restored dewpond and a couple of seats with the unusual inscription 'Please give up this seat for a young person'.

Cissbury Ring.

Coombes Church.

Walk 14

SPRINGHEAD HILL, CLAPHAM AND MICHELGROVE

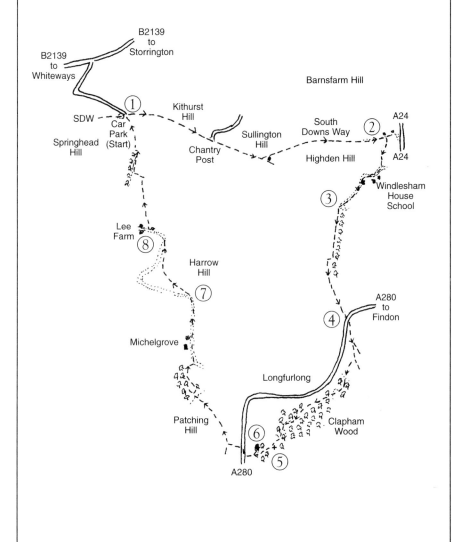

Walk 14

SPRINGHEAD HILL, CLAPHAM AND MICHELGROVE

Distance:	11¾ miles
Route:	Springhead Hill - South Downs Way - Chantry Post - Highden Hill - Windlesham House School - Highden Barn - Clapham Wood - Clapham Church - Patching Hill - Michelgrove - Harrow Hill - Lee Farm - Springhead Hill.
Map:	OS Explorer 121: Arundel and Pulborough
Start/Parking:	From the B2139 Storrington-to-Whiteways road about 1½ miles from Storrington follow a No Through Road (unsigned) southwards up to the summit of the Downs. Park in the Springhead Hill car park on the right at the top of the hill. GR 070124.
Public Transport:	None
Conditions:	An undulating walk, all on good tracks or paths, some of which may be muddy after rain.
Refreshments:	None on the route.

From a starting point high on the Downs to the east of the Arun valley this walk follows a glorious open section of the South Downs Way before heading south on the western slopes of the Findon valley. After contouring round the hillside above the Longfurlong, a woodland path drops down to visit the lovely little secluded flint-built church at Clapham. The return route takes an undulating course across low hills, gradually gaining height to regain the summit of the Downs escarpment once more. It is a fine walk mainly across open downland, allowing good steady progress with few stiles and fairly gentle ups and downs.

The path down from Sullington Hill.

THE WALK

From the entrance to the car park **(1)** turn right through a gate, then left along a clear track, signposted as the South Downs Way. Continue past Chantry Post where there is another car park and forward, soon on an unfenced track across Sullington Hill. On reaching a barn, keep left, leaving the barn on your right. Carry on over Barnsfarm Hill, ignoring the signed alternative route for the South Downs Way which goes off to the left.

The views are superb throughout - northwards across the Weald to the distant Surrey Hills, as well as ahead along the line of the South Downs to Chanctonbury Hill on the other side of the valley crowned by the depleted remains of the tree clump on Chanctonbury Ring.

After another three quarters of a mile, soon after the track becomes a metalled drive, at a point when you are opposite the access drive to Bostal Hill House on your left **(2)**, turn right along a tree-lined bridleway. Join and go ahead along an access drive with the buildings of Windlesham House School to your left. Where the drive divides, keep left past some cottages, still on a drive, signed as a Private Road, though it is also a public bridleway.

Just before the drive bears away to the left (3) go right along a track for 20 yards, then left along a headland path with a strip of woodland on your left. Where the path divides, sidestep to the right through a gap in the hedge and turn left, resuming your previous direction, still along a left field edge with trees to your left. At a concrete crossing track turn right and after 60 yards go left along a wide grassy track.

From here there is a good view to the left across the Findon Valley to the ramparts of the Iron Age fort on Cissbury Ring (Walk 13).

At the A280 (4) cross the road and follow the track opposite, ignoring an immediate track to the left and climbing obliquely up the hillside. At a way post, fork right on a path which contours along the upper slope of the Longfurlong valley, gradually curving to the right. Where the path divides again, fork right on a path which, after 200 yards or so, enters woodland. Follow signs, waymarks and stiles with care for almost a mile through alternating woodland and cleared areas, finally crossing a meadow to enter Clapham churchyard (5).

The simple 12th to 13th century church is notable for some 16th century brasses of the Shelley family, ancestors of the poet, though it was locked up and inaccessible when I last passed this way, a sad sign of the times.

Leave the churchyard through the main gate, bear left along the church access drive and, after 30 yards, fork right along a woodland path. After leaving the wood over a stile, drop down along a left field edge to join the A280 road with the spire of Patching

Distant view of Cissbury ring from path between points 3 and 4.

church directly in line ahead. *Turn right beside this busy vergeless road (for the sake of safety you might feel inclined to stay, unofficially, within the field to the right of the road). After about 100 yards (6), turn left along a grassy strip which climbs, soon becoming a hollow tree lined path which emerges at a small parking area. Bear right through a gate and, after 10 yards, fork left along a rising track which soon opens out on to the open grassland of Patching Hill.*

Over to your right you now have a good view back across the valley to the path used earlier above Longfurlong and Clapham Wood with Chanctonbury Ring beyond.

Climb, walking parallel to the hedge on your left. After half a mile or so go ahead through a gate into woodland and, after another 100 yards or so, go right on a signed path which soon drops obliquely down along the edge of the wood and on across a field to join a lane.

Turn left and follow this lane gently up past Michelgrove House on the left. After another half a mile where minor power lines converge from the right (7), fork right through a gate and follow a faint unfenced grassy path which crosses the lower left flank of Harrow Hill, walking roughly parallel but well to the left of the aforementioned power lines.

There is, regrettably, no right of access up to the 550 ft summit of Harrow Hill, an important ancient site where over 100 flint mines, dating from about 2000 BC, were excavated and explored in 1924.

View towards Clapham Wood from path near point 4.

On the other side of the hill, a track passes under the power lines and drops down across a field to rejoin the access drive to Lee Farm. Follow this drive round to the left and up towards this large farm complex. Just past a row of cottages and before the main farm buildings **(8)** turn right along a chalk and flint track. Follow this track as it gains height steadily to reach a T-junction

Old W.W.II tank beyond point 8.

of tracks where you should turn left. On reaching a belt of trees turn right and continue with the trees on your left. Ignore the first left fork and, where the trees end, go left along a track for 20 yards, then right through a gap and squarely ahead across a field and on through an area of scrub.

A short detour along a path to the left from this point will bring you to the remains of a World War II tank, a reminder that much of the Downs was requisitioned as an army training area during the war years. Return the same way.

Beyond the belt of scrub head out half left across another large field which is liable to be ploughed out and may not be obvious. As you cross a low rise the car park and the end of the walk come into sight in the far left field corner.

Clapham Church, point 5.

Walk 15
BIGNOR HILL, SLINDON AND STANE STREET

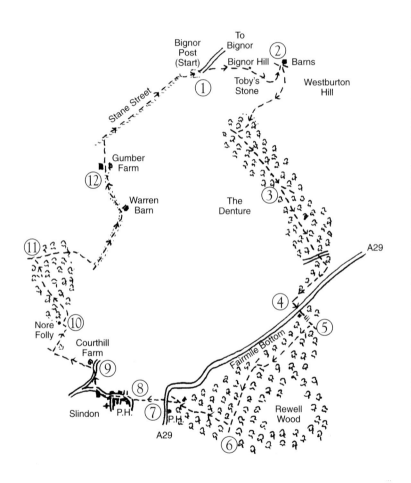

Walk 15
BIGNOR HILL, SLINDON AND STANE STREET

Distance:	11 miles
Route:	Bignor Post - Westburton Hill - The Denture - Fairmile Bottom - Rewell Wood -Slindon - Nore Folly - Gumber Farm - Stane Street - Bignor Post.
Map:	OS Explorer 121 - Arundel and Pulborough
Start/Parking:	At Bignor Post, reached via a narrow road from the village of Bignor which is most easily accessible westwards along a narrow lane from the A29 about 2 miles north of Whiteways. Park in the large parking area at the top of the Downs escarpment at GR 974129.
Public Transport:	None
Conditions:	A straightforward walk mostly using firm downland tracks and woodland paths. Gently undulating except for one steep climb up into Rewell Wood.
Refreshments:	Newburgh Arms pub at Slindon

Much of this walk lies within the 3500 acre Slindon Estate. Although owned by the National Trust, there is limited open public access as much of the area is farmed, and it is necessary to rely on the reasonable network of public rights of way. Although it starts across high open downland with superb open views, much of this circuit lies within woodland, reminding us of the densely afforested nature of large areas within the West Sussex Downs.

From a high point on Bignor Hill at over 700 ft above sea level the walk descends almost to the level of the coastal plain to visit the picturesque flint built village of Slindon where there is a well placed pub about half way round the circuit. A long and fairly gentle climb then brings us in stages back up to the summit of the Downs. As a grand finale, the walk follows a well preserved section of the Roman road known as Stane Street which once linked London with Chichester.

THE WALK

From the car park *(1)* start the walk eastwards along the South Downs Way as it forks right from the top of the road leading up from the valley and climbs, unfenced, over Bignor Hill.

As you cross the summit area a fine view opens up ahead along the line of the Downs escarpment as far as Wolstonbury Hill (Walk 1). On your left you will pass Toby's Stone, a memorial to a local huntsman, now in ruins though an attempt has been made to piece together the fragments of the inscription.

Continue with this track as it drops down, doubling sharply back to the left. About 100 yards short of a triple barn *(2)*, leave the South Downs Way by turning sharply back to the right on a grassy track with a fence on your right at first which continues as a fine terraced path across the shoulder of Bignor Hill before dropping down again across a large field, passing through a dip to enter woodland. A few yards inside the wood, ignore a right fork and climb steadily. Go straight over an unsigned crossing path and, at a T-junction with a wide track, turn left.

Ignore the first signed bridleway to the right, marked with a finger post. After another 200 yards you will come to a way post with blue arrows indicating another division of bridleways. Fork right here *(3)*. After a little over half a mile go straight across a lane and follow the bridleway opposite which drops down through pleasant woodland before bearing right along the valley within earshot of the A29 road, away to your left. Ignore a left fork and, after another half mile or so, bear left with the path up to join the main road *(4)*.

Turn left and after a few yards go right through the entrance to a car park, passing to the left of a wooden building, once a small café but currently empty and boarded up.

This is the starting point for a Nature Trail exploring a 120-acre public open space, embracing chalk grassland and wooded slopes of predominantly beech and yew. Our walk uses part of the Trail.

Go right behind the building and, after a few yards, left to follow a steep path up through woodland, aided by steps. At the top some care is needed as there are several alternative paths and it is easy to go astray. About 30 yards short of a gate *(5)*, turn right along an unsigned path and, immediately, fork left along a narrower path which winds through a coppice and continues parallel and to the right of a low earth bank. Fairly soon the path bears left over the bank and resumes its previous direction with the bank now to the right. Where a path feeds in from the left go ahead on a more substantial path, still beside the bank.

As well as the low boundary bank which guides us, there are numerous other earth works within the wood. It has been suggested that the area might once have been the site of a kind of Celtic city.

Go straight over a crossing path. At a meeting of a number of ways where there is *a way post, go ahead on the path which starts immediately to the left of the post, now once more on a waymarked bridleway. A few yards beyond a wooden barrier, at a meeting of several paths (6), turn squarely right along a signed bridleway. Go over a crossing path and follow a clear track downhill.*

When opposite a scouting activity centre on your right, fork left up through trees to a stile and go ahead on a stiled path across two paddocks to join the A29 (7). Cross the road and climb the steps opposite. A clear path continues out to join a lane beside the Newburgh Arms at Slindon (8). Bear right along the village street, ignoring a road to the right and two other turnings to the left.

The second lane on the left leads to the church and village pond, well worth a short detour. The church is notable for the rare carved wooden effigy of a 16th century knight in armour. The pond is a delightful spot with a path beside it leading in to the National Trust Slindon Woods, once a noble beech plantation until largely flattened in the Great Gale of 1987. Replanting is now well under way.

Carry on out of the village passing Slindon College on your left. Beyond the college entrance follow the lane round to the left and, after a few yards, just short of the road speed de-restriction sign, turn right along an unsigned path which drops down through woodland to join a lane where you should bear right.

After less than 100 yards (9), a few yards short of the buildings of Courthill Farm,

Slindon Church.

Slindon Pond.

fork left along a wide track signed as a public footpath. After a little under half a mile turn right and follow a clear path which climbs steadily beside fields. At the top of the rise go left over a stile and after a few yards, right along a gravel track **(10)**.

At this point a stile provides access to Nore Folly where there is a trig point and a well placed seat with a grandstand prospect over the coastal plain to the south and, on clear days, a distant view of the Isle of Wight. The Folly, built as a summer house for shooting lunches, is now a picturesque flint ruin.

Follow the track to enter Nore Wood where you should go ahead, ignoring two paths to the left. Where the ground begins to drop away ahead, follow the path round to the left and, after a few yards fork right on a track which drops obliquely down the wooded slope. Towards the bottom of the hill, at a junction of tracks **(11)** *turn right and, ignoring a right fork, follow a straight track through a dip with an elegant grove of tall and slender beech trees to your left.*

Where the wood ends go over a crossing track and ahead between fences. After a little over a quarter of a mile turn left and head north along a hard track. Go straight over a crossing bridleway. About 100 yards short of Warren Barn follow the track as it bears round to the left and climbs steadily for another half a mile to reach Gumber Farm **(12)**.

Away to the left of the path, one of the farm buildings has been converted into an overnight camping barn for users of the South Downs Way, well equipped with dormitories and kitchen. It is open during the summer months.

Beyond the farm, go ahead beside a fence for about 200 yards to join the line of Stane Street through a gate where you should turn right and climb, walking either on or beside a well preserved section of the bank or Roman agger. Beyond a gate go straight ahead past a pole barrier and along a track which takes you straight back to the start.

Nore Folly.

The path near point 3.

Walk 16
EARTHAM, EAST DEAN AND GRAFFHAM DOWN

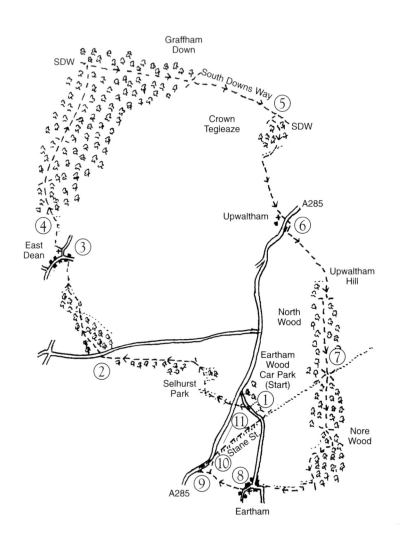

Walk 16

EARTHAM, EAST DEAN AND GRAFFHAM DOWN

Distance:	14 miles.
Route:	Eartham Wood - Selhurst Park - East Dean - South Downs Way - Graffham Down - Crown Tegleaze - Upwaltham - North Wood - Eartham - Stane Street - Eartham Wood.
Map:	OS Explorer 121: Arundel and Pulborough
Start/Parking:	At the Eartham Wood Forestry Commission car park. Heading south along the A285 Petworth-to-Chichester road about seven miles from Chichester, fork left. The car park and picnic area is on the left after half a mile at GR 939106.
Public Transport:	None convenient
Conditions:	Good walking, much of it along firm chalk and flint tracks. Fairly hilly.
Refreshments:	Hurdlemakers pub at East Dean, George Inn at Eartham.

From a starting point on the lower dip slope of the Downs, this walk takes us up to the highest point on the West Sussex Downs at Crown Tegleaze, diverting en route to visit the tiny flint-built village of East Dean, tucked away in a sheltered fold of the Downs. From here a steady but easy climb through woodland brings us up to the summit of the Downs and a two-mile stretch of the South Downs Way across Graffham Down.

The return route re-crosses the valley at Upwaltham before traversing more woodland to reach the village of Eartham where there is a well-placed pub about a mile from the end of the walk.

Although one of the longest walks in the book, the 'going' is invariably good, mostly on firm tracks or good woodland paths and the gradients, although fairly long and frequent, are never too taxing.

THE WALK

From the entrance to the car park (1) turn right along the road. After 250 yards fork left along a signed woodland path. Cross the A285 road and go ahead along the track opposite. After a quarter of a mile turn right over a stile and head out across a large field, aiming for the left hand corner of woodland. On reaching the trees go forward with the wood on your right for 30 yards, then continue beside the wood for another 40 yards before veering half left across grass to a stile, in sight.

Go forward along the lower left edge of a large field, ignoring a signed path to the right. Ignore a stile on your left and, in the field corner, go forward over another stile and ahead through newly planted woodland. Follow a path, stiled and signposted, westwards through the wood for two thirds of a mile. Just short of a car parking area go right over a bank to join a road (2), go right for a few yards, then left past a pole barrier and forward on a woodland track.

After 300 yards or so, at a waypost, fork right, still on a woodland path. Leave the wood over a stile and go ahead across a field to re-enter woodland over another stile,

East Dean village from the path between points 2 and 3.

Follow a clear path through the wood, descending to a T-junction with a bridleway where you should turn right. Leave the wood and continue down between fields. Join an enclosed track, turn left for a few yards, then go right over a stile and forward beside playing fields to join a lane. Turn left. After 150 yards or so the walk continues to the right along Newhouse Lane (3).

If time allows the lane ahead leads down into the compact little brick and flint village of East Dean, well worth the short detour, particularly if you are in need of sustenance as the Hurdlemakers Inn provides a warm welcome for walkers. The tiny church is much restored but, in part, dates from the 13th century.

Where Newhouse Lane veers round to the right, fork left along a chalk track. A few yards along this track is a convenient access on the left to East Dean church. Our track climbs steadily between high banks. Shortly after it opens out on to grass downland, fork right at a waypost and continue up, now within a grassy hollow which leads up past a wooden seat and on, soon along a right field edge. As you approach the field corner ignore a signed path to the right and, after another 40 yards (4) go ahead through a bridle gate and ahead on a clear path which contours along the wooded hillside through a maturing beech plantation.

Where the path divides, fork right on the lower path which takes an almost straight course for about 1½ miles during which you should ignore all side and crossing paths. At a T-junction with the South Downs Way, turn right and follow it for another 1½ miles, once again ignoring side and crossing paths. Enclosed at first with restricted views, it eventually opens out on to Graffham Down, passing a substantial carved oak post commemorating Edmund Barkworth, a stalwart conservationist and distinguished member of the Society of Sussex Downsmen.

The post overlooks an area which was the focus of a major furore in the early '80s when a Dutch farmer ploughed up an important wildlife habitat, embracing 120 acres of trees, scrub and precious traditional chalk downland. Ironically the owner sold up and left the area within a few years, but the damage was done.

On reaching another solid carved oak post erected by the Cowdray Hunt in 1972, once with four arms, now reduced to two, turn sharply back to the right, signed to East Dean (5), parting company with the South Downs Way. After 100 yards or so, fork left along a wide grassy woodland track, signed as a bridleway. Ignore two paths to the right, leave the wood through a bridle gate next to a gnarled beech tree and turn right along the right edge of a field.

You are now within a few yards of the highest point on the West Sussex Downs, at 830 ft above sea level. As a vantage point it is disappointing because of the surrounding trees, cutting off the views on three sides and has no trig point or other marker.

After about 250 yards, at a T-junction, turn left and follow an unfenced track across high open downland and down to join the A285 at the tiny settlement of Upwaltham.

On the right, just short of the road, is the Norman church, relatively unaltered since the 12th century.

Cross the road **(6)**, go through a bridle gate, almost opposite, and head half right across a meadow. On reaching the first buildings of Upwaltham Farm on your right, go left through a second bridle gate and follow a fence on your left steadily up on to the Downs, soon between low banks. A wide track, fenced at first continues up and over Upwaltham Hill and on into woodland.

At a T-junction with a wide crossing track turn right and after 40 yards go left along a wide track which drops steadily downhill through woodland for over half a mile to reach a meeting point of seven ways **(7)** where Stane Street crosses and there is another specially carved oak signpost. Go virtually straight ahead here on a wide forest path which starts to the right of a 'No Horses' notice.

After another half a mile, just past a pole barrier go over a crossing track and ahead on a track which climbs obliquely up a wooded hillside, duplicating, though in the opposite direction, a short section of Walk 15. Towards the top of the hill turn sharply back to the right, still on a clear track. Follow this track across the wooded summit of Nore Hill, eventually heading generally southwards.

East Dean village green and pond.

After a little over a quarter of a mile, turn right over a stile, leaving the wood to follow a right field edge. In the field corner, turn left, still within the same field and, after a little over 100 yards go right through a wide gap and forward on a headland track which takes you out to the road at Eartham.

East Dean Church.

Go directly ahead along the road. At a road junction with the George Inn a few yards away to your right, you should fork left. Shortly, opposite the church on your left **(8),** *fork right along a track which starts to the right of a house called the Old Vicarage. Your path continues across a dip following an intermittent line of Scots Pines. Beyond a kissing gate, where there is a choice of waymarked paths, go directly ahead over the summit of Long Down. Beyond the highest point the path officially veers slightly right across open downland. If ploughed out or cultivated you may find it easier to follow a fence down and round to the right along the field edge.*

Both routes bring you to a stile **(9)** *where the official route goes ahead over a second stile and down to join the A285 road. (To avoid a dangerous section of main road it is possible to go right here for 200 yards beside a fence direct to point 11. This is not a right of way but is unlikely to interfere with farming activities so would seem to be a reasonable short cut in the interests of safety). If using the official route, turn right beside the main road where there is a reasonable verge on the left and good sight lines and, after 250 yards fork right over a stile* **(10)** *where the short cut rejoins. Now follow the raised bank of Stane Street to a second stile, soon in sight and on through scrub, climbing and then dropping down.*

The Roman road known as Stane Street was constructed in A.D.70 to link Chichester with London. It consisted of a raised bank or agger flanked by ditches and was up to 25 ft wide in places. From here it can be followed, using official rights of way for four miles up to Bignor Post. Although here obscured by trees and scrub, a more open and less overgrown section is followed on Walk 15.

Continue with Stane Street, ignoring crossing tracks, for over half a mile out to a road. Follow the forestry road into Eartham Wood opposite. After a few yards, where Stane Street goes ahead, fork left and after a few more yards go left along a wide path for a short distance back to the car park.

Walk 17
BOW HILL AND THE MARDENS

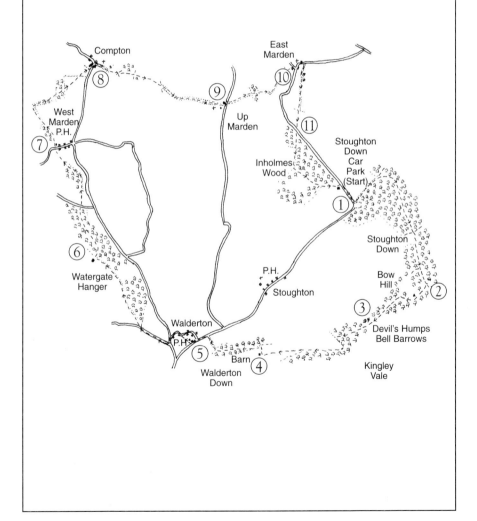

Walk 17
BOW HILL AND THE MARDENS

Distance:	12 miles
Route:	Stoughton Down FC car park - Stoughton Down - Bow Hill - Walderton - Watergate Hanger - West Marden - Compton - Up Marden - East Marden - Stoughton Down FC car park.
Map:	OS Explorer 120: Chichester
Start/Parking:	At the Stoughton Down Forestry Commission car park (GR 815126). Access is along quiet lanes, either from the B2141 Chichester-to-South Harting road north of Chilgrove via East Marden or from the B2147/2146 Emsworth-to-South Harting road at Walderton via Stoughton.
Public Transport:	None convenient
Conditions:	Excellent walking along clear paths and tracks. One steady climb and plenty of intermediate ups and downs, also one short sharp descent which may be slippery after rain.
Refreshments:	Pubs at Walderton, West Marden (just off the route) and Compton.

To the north west of Chichester, where the long thin strip of the Sussex Downs is at its broadest, lies the thinly populated area of rolling hills explored on this rather special walk, one of my favourites. It crosses a patchwork of downs and woodland, including traverses through several fine beech hangers, and links five small villages, including Up Marden with its remote and unspoilt church and East Marden, notable for an attractive thatched well-head and another lovely old flint-walled church. In spite of their remote location, three of the villages have pubs, all offering excellent food and good beer and there is a village shop at Compton. The walk starts with a steady climb up on to the 600 ft ridge of Bow Hill, with exceptional views. It then circles to the north, with a number of ups and downs, though none are too long or severe, except one sharp and potentially slippery descent through woodland beyond Up Marden.

THE WALK

Start the walk along a gravel track which begins past a metal barrier at the bottom corner of the car park **(1)**. *Ignore a left fork, continuing along the main track through mature beech wood, soon beginning to climb gently. Where the track divides again, keep right (straight on). Where you come out into the open at a meeting of a number of ways, go ahead, still on a gravel track with woodland to your left.*

A fine view opens out briefly to the right down the valley towards Stoughton and Walderton.

After a little over 100 yards, at a waypost, fork left along a narrower path which plunges back into woodland where the beech gives way in places to scattered yew. Ignore the first waymarked path to the right, but after another 250 yards, at a Kingley Vale National Nature Reserve notice **(2)**, *fork right along a wide crossing track.*

The Reserve, apart from its 30,000 yew trees, reputedly the largest yew forest in Europe, incorporates areas of chalk downland and manages to support a wide variety of chalk downland flowers and butterflies.

East Marden - Church and well-head.

Beech Woods near West Marden.

Follow this track, passing the trig point on the highest point on Bow Hill (675 ft) hidden obscurely away in the scrub to the right of the path without views. Despair not, however. Carry on along the track until it comes out on to open grass downland with magnificent views to the left across Kingley Vale towards Chichester harbour and the sea. Carry on along the track, passing about 40 yards to the left of two striking bell barrows known as the Devil's Humps (3). Allow time for a short detour up on to one of them where you get a commanding view across a wide expanse of rolling downland to the north.

Go straight over a crossing track beside another nature reserve notice. At a T-junction on the edge of the wood turn sharply back to the left. After 100 yards, at a path junction, turn right on a track which follows the edge of a dense yew wood, then through the trees and on, between fences, across open downland with more wide views.

At a ruined barn (4), turn right and, on reaching the edge of woodland, turn left to follow a path and then a track obliquely down through a beech hanger. Towards the bottom of the hill, go ahead past a Forestry Commission notice and on out to a lane where you should turn left into Walderton. A few yards past the Barley Mow pub (5) turn right along a drive past Primrose Cottage. It becomes a path which crosses the tiny River Ems, a winterbourne, normally dry during the summer, and continues out to a lane.

Turn left and, at a junction with the B2146, turn left again. Shortly fork right along a slip road and right again along a narrow lane. Follow this quiet cul-de-sac steadily uphill, soon between high banks until, after about a quarter of a mile, you can fork right along a rough track and shortly, where it divides, fork left to follow a track for half a mile along the top edge of Watergate Hanger. Where the track divides again, keep left, still above the wood. At a T-junction next to a flint house **(6)**, turn right into woodland. After 30 yards, at a junction of tracks, go straight ahead on a flinty track which curves left within the hanger, level at first, then losing height. Where the track divides, keep right, go straight over a drive, cross a lane and go over the stile opposite.

Now follow a stiled path at the foot of a grassy slope, forward along the left edge of a field, back into the wood on your left and on within the lower wood edge. Finally go forward across two paddocks and out to a lane at West Marden **(7)**.

If in need of refreshment, the nucleus of the village and the Victoria Inn are along the lane to the right.

Our walk continues to the left along the lane and, almost immediately, right along the drive to a house called Marden Down. After a few yards a narrow path, starting to the left of the house gateway, squeezes to the left of the house and garden and continues on a level course along a wooded slope. After leaving the wood, go ahead

Compton village square, new well-head and village shop.

Barley Mow Inn, Walderton

along a right field edge until, after 150 yards, you can turn right over a stile and ahead on a fenced track up a short sharp incline.

At the top you have a choice of three signed paths. Yours is the one in the middle which bears half left on a normally trodden out route across the middle of a cultivated field, then on through an area of young trees and scrub surrounded by a deer fence where gates are provided in this high barrier. Continue in the same direction down across a field corner, through a line of pine trees and on across the next field to join the B2146 road. Turn left into Compton. Immediately beyond the Coach and Horses pub **(8)**, turn right along a lane.

The pub, which makes walkers welcome in its cosy 'village bar', faces the village shop across the small square. The elegant well-head in the middle of the square is new, constructed as a millennium project by students from the Chichester College of Arts, Science and Technology.

Where the lane narrows to a track you can gain access to the neat little flint church up steps on your left. Carry on up the track and, shortly, at a waypost, fork left and, after a few yards, go ahead over a stile beside a gate and steeply uphill along the left edge of two fields.

At the top, pause to catch your breath and to look back across the valley where you can pick out most of your route over the hill from West Marden to Compton.

In the top field corner go half left along a track and, after 20 yards at a four-arm sign, bear right along a track, walking beneath minor power lines. Follow this track as it descends into another valley and climbs again, shaded by trees, for the best part of a mile, to reach the hamlet of Up Marden.

The tiny church, one of the most beautiful and atmospheric of all downland churches, can be reached along a short grassy path to the right at the top of the hill.

Continue out to a lane **(9)** and turn left past the converted farm buildings at Up Marden Farm on your left. After 100 yards, turn right along a grassy track and after 60 yards, go forward with a hedge on your right. From the field corner a path, slippery in places, drops steeply down through a wood, Go straight over a crossing path, leave the wood over a stile and go forward along a right field edge. In the field corner go over a stile and turn right round two sides of a field. After about 350 yards go half right over a stile and across the middle of a field to join a lane. Turn right into East Marden.

At a junction next to the attractive thatched well-head **(10)**, turn left, passing, on your left, another modest flint-built downland church. After another 100 yards, turn right opposite the parish notice board and along a farm access drive. Follow this drive round to the left. A few yards past a milking parlour on your right, turn right over a barway to the right of a double gate and go ahead, passing two barns on your left, to

View from beyond Walderton.

find a stile. Continue along the right edge of one field and the left edge of two more fields before veering slightly left across a third field out to a lane **(11)**.

Turn left and immediately fork right along a track which climbs steadily up through beech woodland and on along a left field edge. In the field corner turn left, back into the wood. Follow a clear path through the wood and down to join a lane via the access drive from Wildham Barn. Turn right back to the start.

Bell Barrow, Bow Hill

Walk 18
STANSTED FOREST, CHALTON AND WEST HARTING DOWN

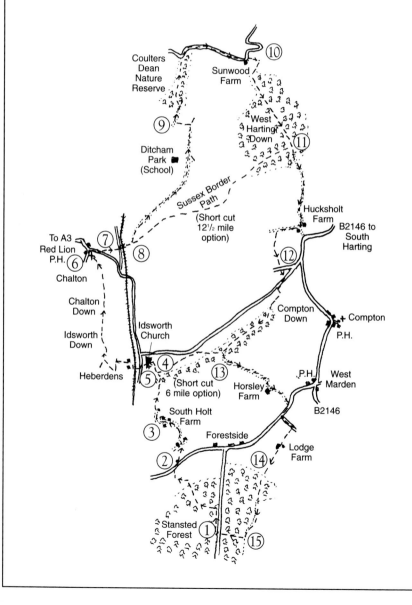

Walk 18
STANSTED FOREST, CHALTON AND WEST HARTING DOWN

Distance:	15 miles
Route:	Stansted Forest - South Holt Farm -Idsworth Church - Chalton Down - Chalton - Ditcham Park - Coulters Dean - South Downs Way - Sunwood Farm - West Harting Down - Hucksholt Farm - Compton Down - Horsley Farm - Lodge Farm - Stansted Forest.
Map:	OS Explorer 120 - Chichester
Start/Parking:	At Stansted Forest to the north of Emsworth. Park in the middle of three car parking areas marked on the Explorer map beside the north-south road through the Forest. GR 754111.
Public Transport:	None
Conditions:	An undulating route mostly on clear tracks or across open downland. The track across West Harting Down may be churned up and muddy due to timber hauling.
Refreshments:	Red Lion pub at Chalton after the first 4½ miles.

This is a substantial full day walk, straddling the county boundary between West Sussex and Hampshire and exploring the rolling dip slope of the Downs. Although predominantly a West Sussex walk, it strays across the border into Hampshire to visit the isolated church at Idsworth, followed by a fine ridge walk across Chalton Down to reach the charming little village of Chalton where the Red Lion pub provides welcome refreshment. After a steady climb to the top of the Downs escarpment the return route traverses the high afforested area of West Harting Down.

The walk can be shortened, either to 6 miles by using a valley and woodland path between points 4 and 13 or by using the Sussex Border Path, marked on the Explorer map between points 8 and 11. Neither of these short cuts is described in detail in the text so a map is essential if you are hoping to use either of these shorter options.

THE WALK

From the northern end of the car park (1) start the walk along a permissive horse track which runs parallel and to the left of the road. After about a quarter of a mile, just short of another small car park, turn left along a forest track. Where the track divides, keep straight ahead. At a meeting of five paths, go half right, indicated by a yellow waymark. At the next crossing track go straight ahead and, after 20 yards, fork left, still on a waymarked path.

Leave the forest over a stile, cross a dip to a second stile and turn left along an enclosed path within a belt of scrub. Where the path opens out, go ahead along a left field edge. After 100 yards, bear right to a stile beside a gate, climb across a field to join a road and turn right. After about 200 yards (2) turn left along the drive to a house called Dunsmere and shortly fork right along a narrow path. Beyond the next stile follow telephone lines across a field to a stile from which a path drops down through woodland.

Idsworth Church.

Go over a crossing track and follow another clear track ahead, soon between high hedges. At South Holt Farm **(3)** turn left along a metalled drive, leaving the flint walled farmhouse on your left. Follow this drive round to the right and, after 60 yards, go right along a track laid with concrete strips. Pass to the left of a cottage and, where the track ends at a stile, go half right across two fields with a stile between them to enter woodland over a third stile.

A clear path continues through this attractive area of mixed woodland. Where the path divides, fork left along a path which drops down through the wood and leaves it over a stile. Go forward with a fence on your right, passing a curious circular walled pit (could this be the remains of an ice house?). After about 100 yards go over a stile, forward for 10 yards, then right over a second stile **(4)**. (For the 6-mile walk option follow the path ahead along the valley and up through woodland to rejoin the main walk at point 13).

To continue with the full walk, turn left along the field edge. After 250 yards go left again over a stile and across a field to reach Idsworth Church **(5)**.

St Hubert's Chapel, built in the 11th century, stands in complete isolation on the lower slopes of the valley formed by a winterbourne stream which only comes to life after heavy winter rain. The church is notable for some wall paintings, thought to date from about 1330.

A path continues down, across a wooden causeway over the, usually dry, stream,

Idsworth Church.

and out to a road. Turn left and, after a few yards, right along a farm drive which passes under the railway. Shortly go right and left between the farm buildings at Heberdens' Farm and steadily up onto the Downs. About half way up, follow the track round to the left and, after about 150 yards, turn sharply back to the right, still climbing steadily, now on an unfenced track.

At the top of the hill turn right on a grassy strip which skirts to the right of a block of woodland. Follow the left field edge until you can sidestep to the left over a stile and follow a ridge path which passes to the left of an electricity pylon and heads out along the ridge of Idsworth and Chalton Down, marked by wayposts.

The views from the ridge are second to none - back across the valley and ahead to Butser Hill with its prominent radio mast, the extensive woodland of the Queen Elizabeth Forest and a wide vista of the rolling dip slope of the Downs, rising gradually towards the distant northern escarpment.

Follow this trodden path down to a junction where you should turn left over a stile, across a meadow and out through Chalton churchyard, to join a lane opposite the Red Lion pub **(6)**.

The church dates mainly from the 11th to 13th centuries and the grass in the churchyard is kept trimmed by a resident flock of sheep. The thatched and timber-framed Red Lion pub, built in 1147, lays claim to be the oldest pub in Hampshire.

Red Lion, Chalton.

Turn right and immediately fork right, signposted to Idsworth and Ditcham. Ignore the first two signed paths to the left. After 250 yards, just short of the top of the hill go left through a gap in the hedge and bear half right across a field where the path is once again marked out by wooden posts. Go over two stiles and drop steeply down a grassy slope and out via a short enclosed path to join a lane (7).

Turn left and, after a few yards, right across a railway footbridge and forward along a farm track. Go over a crossing track and along another track ahead. Shortly, just past a cottage on the left (8), fork left along a fenced track. (For the 12½-mile walk option, a right fork here is the start of a two-mile link along the Sussex Border Path to point 11). For the full 15-mile walk follow the aforementioned fenced track as it rises gradually for over a mile, eventually passing Ditcham Park School, over to the left. Go ahead along the school access drive until, after 350 yards, you can turn left along a path, signed as a bridleway, beside a wooded strip.

At a junction with a forest track (9), turn right and after about 250 yards, fork left on a path marked by blue painted posts, which soon passes along the side of a delightful beech hanger to enter Coulters Dean Nature Reserve.

The Reserve, managed by the Hampshire Wildlife Trust, partly woodland and partly chalk downland is, as a notice reminds us, a valuable site for wild flowers, including several types of orchid and the Round Head Rampion, as well as a number of butterfly species, notably the Marbled White and the locally rare Duke of Burgundy Fritillary.

Follow this path out to a lane and turn right, now on part of the South Downs Way. After half a mile, at Sunwood Farm, follow the lane round to the left and, after 60 yards, fork right along an unmade track, still with the South Downs Way. At the top of a rise (10), where there is a wide view northwards into the Weald, turn right along a clear signed bridleway, parting company with the South Downs Way.

On entering woodland, stick to the signed bridleway, ignoring a left fork. A wide forest track takes a straight course across West Harting Down where you should ignore all side and crossing tracks. After two thirds of a mile (11) you will cross the signed Sussex Border Path where the 12½-mile walk option joins from the right, directly from point 8. Where the wood comes to an end on your right, fork right along a narrower hedged path.

After another half mile or so, at Hucksholt Farm, where the track becomes a metalled drive, turn right along a narrow lane which gains height gradually. After about 500 yards go left through a squeeze stile and forward along a left field edge. In the field corner pass through two more squeeze stiles and veer slightly left across a field to join a lane (12). Go through another squeeze stile, opposite, and maintain your previous direction across a field to join another lane. Turn right.

After 150 yards go left through a gate and right, walking parallel to the lane. In the field corner follow the fence round to the left until you can go right through a gate. A

faint path goes ahead, contouring along the hillside to a gate and on along a good track.
From this path there are good views across the valley to Chalton Down.
Looking back along the path you get a glimpse of the 17th century mansion at
Uppark, now in the hands of the National Trust and open to the public during
the summer months.

Beyond a second gate a wide track climbs obliquely up through woodland
and, at the top, goes ahead, still within the wood. Ignore a signed path to the left and
another to the right. After a few yards, at a junction, bear left. (At the edge of the
wood (13), the shorter 6-mile walk joins from the right, direct from point 4).

Continue along the main track for the best part of a mile, past Horsley Farm and
out to a road where you should turn right. Take the first turning on the left, signposted
to Walderton and, after about 250 yards, go right along a fenced path which takes a
straight route past Lodge Farm and on across a field to enter Stansted Forest (14).
Stansted Forest covers over 1000 acres of mixed broad-leaved woodland

Chalton Church.

intermingled with chestnut coppice and areas of planted conifers. It can be explored using a network of rights of way as well as permitted paths and tracks.

Go forward on a signed bridleway through the forest, ignoring other paths. After it leaves the wood, go right along the edge of the forest. After another quarter of a mile **(15)** go right over a stile and follow a footpath, marked with yellow arrows, which goes left and right, then heads steadily westwards through the forest to reach the road opposite the start of the walk.

ABOUT THE AUTHOR

Ben Perkins was born in the village of Rodmell, near Lewes and has lived, worked and walked in Sussex throughout his life. He is a keen conservationist and longstanding member of the Society of Sussex Downsmen, Society of Sussex Wealdmen and the Ramblers' Association. Over the last 15 years he has contributed more than 400 walk descriptions to a regular column in the Brighton Evening Argus and during that time has managed to explore much of the 2000 mile network of local footpaths and bridleways.

S.B. Publications publish a wide range of local interest books on Sussex.
For a free catalogue please write to:
S.B. Publications, 19 Grove Road, Seaford, East Sussex BN25 1TP
or access our website on
www.sbpublications.swinternet.co.uk